St. Louis Community College

Forest Park
Florissant Valley
Meramec

Instructional Resources
St. Louis, Missouri

FIFTY YEARS AFTER THE DECLARATION

The United Nations' Record on Human Rights

Edited by

Teresa Wagner
Leslie Carbone

University Press of America,® Inc.   Family Research Council
Lanham · New York · Oxford   Washington, D. C.

Copyright © 2001 by
University Press of America,® Inc.
4720 Boston Way
Lanham, Maryland 20706

12 Hid's Copse Rd.
Cumnor Hill, Oxford OX2 9JJ

Library of Congress Cataloging-in-Publication Data

ISBN 0-7618-1841-3 (cloth : alk. ppr.)
ISBN 0-7618-1842-1 (paper : alk. ppr.)

CONTENTS

Preface

A First Step

Teresa R. Wagner, Editor

The Family Research Council recognizes the United Nations' 1948 Universal Declaration of Human Rights, like the Declaration of Independence before it, as a fundamental statement of the unalienable and transcendent rights of the human person. Indeed, the very notion of "human rights," which exist before and beyond government, acknowledges the transcendent dimension of man, thus implicitly acknowledging man's origins in God.

In recent years, however, the Declaration has become a tool for those who would reduce man to a material, autonomous self, necessarily preoccupied with his own wants. It has been invoked, for example, not so much to protect "life, liberty and security of person" (Article 3), as to advance abortion, homosexuality, euthanasia and other destructive causes, which invariably victimize some human beings for the benefit of others. It is ever thus with materialist man, who becomes oblivious not only to God, but also, ultimately, to his fellow man.

It is with some sadness, therefore, that the Family Research Council produces *Fifty Years After the Declaration*. Compiled from essays written in 1998 to commemorate the fiftieth anniversary of the Declaration, this book illustrates the degree to which the Declaration's ideals have been subverted. Though the Declaration continues to inspire and teach with practical effect in many countries, the papers herein make painfully clear that its ideals have been not only unfulfilled, but even betrayed in many instances by those who would "reinterpret" (that is, pervert) its meaning.

Family Research Council is all too familiar with this type of "reinterpretation." Abortion advocates in America, for example, knew that most citizens would reject abortion as a "right" and that this practice would become acceptable only if initially imposed from above. Thus was the United States Constitution "interpreted" to encompass the so-called abortion right, a travesty of justice that normal political channels could not correct, since those interpreting the Constitution are far removed from the people, neither representing nor answering to the body politic.

The success of this "reinterpretation" strategy in American legal institutions need not be reviewed in depth here. But exposing this strategy at the United Nations—also an institution removed from the people—is the purpose of this book. One hopes it is not too late to stem the tide there and to call member nations back to the Declaration's original vision and promise.

The essays in this book mark the beginning of Family Research Council's commitment to bring the United Nations back in this direction. They leave no doubt that such a turnaround will be a long and difficult process. But every journey requires a first step. This book is ours.

Universal Declaration of Human Rights

Adopted and Proclaimed by the General Assembly of the United Nations on December 10, 1948

PREAMBLE

Whereas recognition of the inherent dignity and of the equal and inalienable rights of all members of the human family is the foundation of freedom, justice and peace in the world,

Whereas disregard and contempt for human rights have resulted in barbarous acts which have outraged the conscience of mankind, and the advent of a world in which human beings shall enjoy freedom of speech and belief and freedom from fear and want has been proclaimed as the highest aspiration of the common people,

Whereas it is essential, if man is not to be compelled to have recourse, as a last resort, to rebellion against tyranny and oppression, that human rights should be protected by the rule of law,

Whereas it is essential to promote the development of friendly relations between nations,

Whereas the peoples of the United Nations have in the Charter reaffirmed their faith in fundamental human rights, in the dignity and worth of the human person and in the equal rights of men and women and have determined to promote social progress and better standards of life in larger freedom,

Whereas Member States have pledged themselves to achieve, in co-operation with the United Nations, the promotion of universal respect for and observance of human rights and fundamental freedoms,

Whereas a common understanding of these rights and freedoms is of the greatest importance for the full realization of this pledge,

Now, Therefore THE GENERAL ASSEMBLY proclaims THIS UNIVERSAL DECLARATION OF HUMAN RIGHTS as a common standard of achievement for all peoples and all nations, to the end that every individual and every organ of society, keeping this Declaration constantly in mind, shall strive by teaching and education to promote respect for these rights and freedoms and by progressive measures, national and international, to secure their universal and effective recognition and observance, both among the peoples of Member States themselves and among the peoples of territories under their jurisdiction.

ARTICLE 1

All human beings are born free and equal in dignity and rights. They are endowed with reason and conscience and should act towards one another in a spirit of brotherhood.

ARTICLE 2

Everyone is entitled to all the rights and freedoms set forth in this Declaration, without distinction of any kind, such as race, colour, sex, language, religion, political or other opinion, national or social origin, property, birth or other status. Furthermore, no distinction shall be made on the basis of the political, jurisdictional or international status of the country or territory to which a person belongs, whether it be independent, trust, non-self-governing or under any other limitation of sovereignty.

ARTICLE 3

Everyone has the right to life, liberty and security of person.

ARTICLE 4

No one shall be held in slavery or servitude; slavery and the slave trade shall be prohibited in all their forms.

ARTICLE 5

No one shall be subjected to torture or to cruel, inhuman or degrading treatment or punishment.

ARTICLE 6

Everyone has the right to recognition everywhere as a person before the law.

ARTICLE 7

All are equal before the law and are entitled without any discrimination to equal protection of the law. All are entitled to equal protection against any discrimination in violation of this Declaration and against any incitement to such discrimination.

ARTICLE 8

Everyone has the right to an effective remedy by the competent national tribunals for acts violating the fundamental rights granted him by the constitution or by law.

ARTICLE 9

No one shall be subjected to arbitrary arrest, detention or exile.

ARTICLE 10

Everyone is entitled in full equality to a fair and public hearing by an independent and impartial tribunal, in the determination of his rights and obligations and of any criminal charge against him.

ARTICLE 11

(1) Everyone charged with a penal offence has the right to be presumed innocent until proved guilty according to law in a public trial at which he has had all the guarantees necessary for his defence.

(2) No one shall be held guilty of any penal offence on account of any act or omission which did not constitute a penal offence, under national or international law, at the time when it was committed. Nor shall a heavier penalty be imposed than the one that was applicable at the time the penal offence was committed.

ARTICLE 12

No one shall be subjected to arbitrary interference with his privacy, family, home or correspondence, nor to attacks upon his honour and reputation. Everyone has the right to the protection of the law against such interference or attacks.

ARTICLE 13

(1) Everyone has the right to freedom of movement and residence within the borders of each state.

(2) Everyone has the right to leave any country, including his own, and to return to his country.

ARTICLE 14

(1) Everyone has the right to seek and to enjoy in other countries asylum from persecution.

(2) This right may not be invoked in the case of prosecutions genuinely arising from non-political crimes or from acts contrary to the purposes and principles of the United Nations.

ARTICLE 15

(1) Everyone has the right to a nationality.

(2) No one shall be arbitrarily deprived of his nationality nor denied the right to change his nationality.

ARTICLE 16

(1) Men and women of full age, without any limitation due to race, nationality or religion, have the right to marry and to found a family. They are entitled to equal rights as to marriage, during marriage and at its dissolution.

(2) Marriage shall be entered into only with the free and full consent of the intending spouses.

(3) The family is the natural and fundamental group unit of society and is entitled to protection by society and the State.

ARTICLE 17

(1) Everyone has the right to own property alone as well as in association with others.

(2) No one shall be arbitrarily deprived of his property.

ARTICLE 18

Everyone has the right to freedom of thought, conscience and religion; this right includes freedom to change his religion or belief, and freedom, either alone or in community with others and in public or private, to manifest his religion or belief in teaching, practice, worship and observance.

ARTICLE 19

Everyone has the right to freedom of opinion and expression; this right includes freedom to hold opinions without interference and to seek, receive and impart information and ideas through any media and regardless of frontiers.

ARTICLE 20

(1) Everyone has the right to freedom of peaceful assembly and association.

(2) No one may be compelled to belong to an association.

ARTICLE 21

(1) Everyone has the right to take part in the government of his country, directly or through freely chosen representatives.
(2) Everyone has the right of equal access to public service in his country.
(3) The will of the people shall be the basis of the authority of government; this will shall be expressed in periodic and genuine elections which shall be by universal and equal suffrage and shall be held by secret vote or by equivalent free voting procedures.

ARTICLE 22

Everyone, as a member of society, has the right to social security and is entitled to realization, through national effort and international co-operation and in accordance with the organization and resources of each State, of the economic, social and cultural rights indispensable for his dignity and the free development of his personality.

ARTICLE 23

(1) Everyone has the right to work, to free choice of employment, to just and favorable conditions of work and to protection against unemployment.
(2) Everyone, without any discrimination, has the right to equal pay for equal work.
(3) Everyone who works has the right to just and favorable remuneration ensuring for himself and his family an existence worthy of human dignity, and supplemented, if necessary, by other means of social protection.
(4) Everyone has the right to form and to join trade unions for the protection of his interests.

ARTICLE 24

Everyone has the right to rest and leisure, including reasonable limitation of working hours and periodic holidays with pay.

ARTICLE 25

(1) Everyone has the right to a standard of living adequate for the health and well-being of himself and of his family, including food, clothing, housing and medical care and necessary social services, and the right to security in the event of unemployment, sickness, disability, widowhood, old age or other lack of livelihood in circumstances beyond his control.

(2) Motherhood and childhood are entitled to special care and assistance. All children, whether born in or out of wedlock, shall enjoy the same social protection.

ARTICLE 26

(1) Everyone has the right to education. Education shall be free, at least in the elementary and fundamental stages. Elementary education shall be compulsory. Technical and professional education shall be made generally available and higher education shall be equally accessible to all on the basis of merit.

(2) Education shall be directed to the full development of the human personality and to the strengthening of respect for human rights and fundamental freedoms. It shall promote understanding, tolerance and friendship among all nations, racial or religious groups, and shall further the activities of the United Nations for the maintenance of peace.

(3) Parents have a prior right to choose the kind of education that shall be given to their children.

ARTICLE 27

(1) Everyone has the right freely to participate in the cultural life of the community, to enjoy the arts and to share in scientific advancement and its benefits.

(2) Everyone has the right to the protection of the moral and material interests resulting from any scientific, literary or artistic production of which he is the author.

ARTICLE 28

Everyone is entitled to a social and international order in which the rights and freedoms set forth in this Declaration can be fully realized.

ARTICLE 29

(1) Everyone has duties to the community in which alone the free and full development of his personality is possible.

(2) In the exercise of his rights and freedoms, everyone shall be subject only to such limitations as are determined by law solely for the purpose of securing due recognition and respect for the rights and freedoms of others and of meeting the just requirements of morality, public order and the general welfare in a democratic society.

(3) These rights and freedoms may in no case be exercised contrary to the purposes and principles of the United Nations.

ARTICLE 30

Nothing in this Declaration may be interpreted as implying for any State, group or person any right to engage in any activity or to perform any act aimed at the destruction of any of the rights and freedoms set forth herein.

Introduction

Fifty Years of the U.N. Declaration of Human Rights

Habib C. Malik

Fifty years ago a set of remarkable men and women gathered at a rare—perhaps unique—moment in history to cobble together painstakingly an international document spelling out precisely why human beings have dignity. This became the Universal Declaration of Human Rights, proclaimed on December 10, 1948, from the United Nations General Assembly's meeting place that fall in Paris.

The rarity of the moment lay in the fact that the enterprise at hand was commenced and narrowly completed in the brief interim between the end of history's most devastating war in 1945 and the acceleration after 1948 of the prolonged period of international tension known as the Cold War. And this odd group of framers embodied in their ranks a breadth of outlooks, ethnic and cultural backgrounds, and clashing temperaments that could legitimately claim to be inclusive of the spectrum of diversity that constitutes the human family. I am proud that Charles Malik, my late father, was one of the most active among them in this worthy and historic undertaking.

Habib C. Malik is a founding member of the Foundation for Human and Humanitarian Rights, an independent, non-governmental organization in Lebanon. He is the son of Former Lebanese Foreign Minister Charles Habib Malik.

With its preamble and its 30 concisely crafted articles, the Universal Declaration stands arguably as the 20th century's single most important international document. Its significance is based on the tangible influence it has had around the world toward promoting the betterment of the human condition in specific contexts. Nearly all the popular movements in the late 1980s and early 1990s throughout Eastern Europe that sought liberation from the shackles of totalitarian communism conducted their struggles under the banner of the Universal Declaration of 1948. Similarly, the release of South Africa from the chains of apartheid and the ushering in of the current era of freedom and democracy under Nelson Mandela occurred, among other things, through the direct inspiration of the same Declaration. Aung San Suu Kyi, the prominent human rights activist and dissident in Burma, also belongs to a long line of fighters against repression in their native lands who drew strength from the legacy of the Declaration. This is a document, in short, that has been alive and influential around the world at crucial periods. Today we are not commemorating a lifeless shrine to rights penned half a century ago by an assembly of self-righteous idealists. Instead, we recognize that many of the non-governmental organizations around the world that battle against human rights abuses were spawned thanks largely to the principles of Universal Declaration.

The rights enumerated in the Declaration are truly universal precisely because they adhere intimately and organically to the very essence of what makes us human, namely that which is prior to the differentiation brought on by gender, color, creed, class, citizenship, geography, and all the rest of the secondary indicators of identity.

Yet recent times have witnessed glaring disappointments, indeed major setbacks, in the march towards a greater respect for human dignity. Cambodia, Lebanon, Rwanda, and the former Yugoslavia are four examples of failure that ought to put civilized societies the world over to shame. The proliferation of international terrorism, in particular the ominous approach of an age when fanaticism resorts to weapons of mass destruction, represents another threat to an otherwise heightened awareness of the nature of rights and the means to protect them. Add to these the ongoing insensitivity of the affluent nations to the deepening plight of impoverished and underdeveloped peoples and countries, and it becomes abundantly clear that an exclusive reliance on progress, science, and technology will not create the elusive earthly utopia preached incessantly by the materialists and secularists. If I am rich and comfortable, yet surrounded on all sides by wretchedness and resentment, I am less secure and ultimately less happy. Caring for the underprivileged represents the core of all humanitarian activity—an important component of safeguarding human rights—and reflects the true meaning of Christian charity.

One disturbing phenomenon gaining ground today can best be described as the systemic hijacking of human rights to serve special interests and to promote dubious agendas of a political and generally secular nature. The authors represented in this series of papers attempt, through a series of succinct and carefully reasoned essays, to throw the spotlight on some of the little noticed areas where gross distortions of human rights concern and activism are taking place. As a result of the liberal fight for so-called "gay" rights, abortion "rights," and other pseudo-rights, under assault are nothing short of society's most precious institutions, such as the family, parent-child relations, and basic traditional morality. It is sad that under the guise of protecting human rights there should be launched—and through the United Nations specifically—a sustained attack on those very rights that were enshrined in the Universal Declaration. However, some have chosen to respond candidly, and this series illustrates a few of these responses.

Elisabeth Gusdek-Petersen, for example, reminds us in her piece that parental rights are indeed human rights. She takes on the radical feminist agenda and exposes the havoc it has wreaked at the United Nations. The twisting of children's rights to mean an unwarranted reduction of parental authority is rejected by Gusdek-Petersen, who writes, "Human beings are never entirely autonomous and isolated, and children, by definition, are precisely not so."

Turning to the issue of population control, David Morrison takes the United Nations to task for losing sight over the decades of the original intention of the framers of the Universal Declaration. They upheld individual rights so forcefully that it is quite clear they would have seen ideologically driven attempts toward population control as bogus. Morrison denounces the sterilization campaigns in China and denounces even more strongly the silence with which they are being met. The United Nations has caved in to "the myths of the population control lobby," with the result that atrocities have occurred with the organization's tacit approval. This is an incredible departure from the Universal Declaration that was voted upon fifty years ago by the same international body.

Also focusing on China, Harry Wu, the prominent human rights activist, describes his 19-year ordeal in forced labor camps known to the Chinese as the *Laogai*. He speaks of the deep-seated fear that the Chinese leaders have of real democracy and human rights. Communism, he says, "virtually requires human rights abuses" in order to thrive. He ends by declaring: "We cannot condemn the atrocities committed in the camps of Hitler and Stalin and continue to ignore the ongoing brutality of the *Laogai*."

A related and equally important issue, particularly for China and the Islamic world, is the question of religious freedom. As Paul Marshall attests in his paper, "Religious freedom is key to protecting other freedoms." This is so because it sets a very intimate part of the individual person beyond the reach of both tyrants and the state in general. Witness the dramatic developments of the late eighties and early nineties in Eastern Europe, in which churches and religious leaders were in the forefront of the confrontation with repression that eventually ended in victories for all freedoms across the board. Marshall surveys religious persecution around the globe and explores how Christians as well as members of other faiths in certain regions are being systematically denied the right to express, and sometimes even to hold, their religious beliefs. He also laments the persistent marginalizing of religious causes and factors underlying human rights abuses worldwide by the secular media. The United Nations ought to remain true to Article 18 of the Universal Declaration and recognize the centrality of religion as a powerful factor in both oppression and liberation.

Two papers, by Irving Tragen and Franziska Haller, deal with the thorny issue of drugs and the United Nations. Only after decades of work have a number of conventions against illicit drug trafficking been adopted by the United Nations and ratified by most governments of the world. As with most intergovernmental protocols in international relations, however, the success or failure of these agreed-upon instruments depends on the will and cooperation of national governments. A new problem now looms on the international scene, namely the legalization of drugs by some of these governments.

Nowhere are rights more trampled on a daily basis than when it comes to the beginning and end of life itself. Abortion and euthanasia are the twin scourges of our age, and they have not gone unnoticed by our diligent researchers. David Alton of the British House of Lords and physician Karel Gunning take on these grave and widespread violations and examine the United Nations' indirect—and sometimes unwitting—encouragement of them. In light of Article 3 of the Universal Declaration, which stresses the sanctity of life ("Everyone has the right to life, liberty and security of person"), how, the writers ask, can practices like abortion and euthanasia be condoned? While the first clearly belongs in the trash heap of shameful human practices alongside genocide and eugenics, the second is a flagrant violation of the

Hippocratic Oath that binds doctors to uphold and safeguard life, all life. Once again, conclude the authors, the United Nations needs to return to the 1948 text, and context, of the Universal Declaration and reaffirm fidelity to its spirit.

Lacking any binding mechanism of implementation on the international level, it is amazing how a mere set of universal moral affirmations could have had such lasting impact. It is a testimony to the power of values and a tribute to the individual and collective conscience that continues to make its presence felt in human affairs. Even the most hardened dictator in today's interconnected world cannot continue to ignore indefinitely the alarms being sounded by the global human rights movement. Organizations such as the United Nations and international non-governmental organizations, by giving the greatest possible publicity to governmental human rights abuses, could, with time, drive such tyrants and the systems of oppression they instate either to change or to implode. No antidote to abuse is more potent than the fresh air of public exposure.

The architects of the Universal Declaration were undoubtedly reacting to the recent horrors of the Second World War. However, they had their gaze firmly fixed on the distant future. Their work was intended to endure the test of time and to override the fickleness of passing fads. The fifty years that have elapsed have shown, if anything, that this brief list of rights and freedoms with its stalwart preamble truly possesses the attribute of timelessness. Whenever practice leads some astray, there stands the Universal Declaration as a beacon signaling the way back home. On this anniversary, we call upon the United Nations and its various agencies to pause and take stock of their activities in light of conformity with the spirit and intent of the Universal Declaration.

Much good around the world has been generated by the tireless work of so many people at the United Nations. One need only mention the areas of peacekeeping, famine relief, education, and economic and social progress, where the United Nations has played a central role worldwide to improve security and advance standards of living. Yet much more remains to be accomplished, and the daunting tasks ahead cannot be approached effectively without men and women at the helm who are truly dedicated in their hearts to the substance of what was proclaimed fifty years ago in the Universal Declaration.

Chapter 1

Religious Freedom and the United Nations' Universal Declaration of Human Rights

Paul Marshall

Nineteen ninety-eight is the fiftieth anniversary of the United Nations' Universal Declaration of Human Rights. This paper discusses the human right to religious freedom. It reviews the importance of this right and whether we, through the United Nations, have done it justice in the past fifty years.

Article 18 of the United Nations' Universal Declaration of Human Rights proclaims: "Everyone has the right to freedom of thought, conscience and religion; this right includes freedom to change his religion or belief, and freedom, either alone or in community with others and in public or private, to manifest his religion or belief in teaching, practice, worship and observance." This Article provides a brief and accurate outline of the essence of religious freedom and is rightly regarded as a great achievement in the history of freedom. No U.N. member nation voted against it.

Paul Marshall, Ph.D., has lectured from China to Sudan and is regarded as a leading authority on religious persecution. Dr. Marshall is an Adjunct Fellow at the Claremont Institute, a Senior Fellow at the Center for Religious Freedom at Freedom House, and an award-winning writer.

THE HISTORY AND IMPORTANCE OF RELIGIOUS FREEDOM

Religious freedom was the first internationally recognized human right in the Western world. Treaties ending the religious wars in 16th- and 17th-century Europe enshrined it. It is the very first right in the Bill of Rights of the United States Constitution, which recognizes that freedom of conscience and belief form the heart of human freedom.

Religious freedom is key to protecting other freedoms: It declares to tyrants that the core of the human person is necessarily and properly beyond their reach. It forces governments to acknowledge loyalties that surpass allegiance to the state. Even today, it is usually churches that challenge—indeed, threaten—authoritarian governments in places such as Africa, Latin America and Asia.[1] In the Islamic world, political dissidence is often in the form of religious movements.[2] Effective leaders for political and moral change, from Gandhi to Martin Luther King, have often been motivated by religious faith. In all these cases, it is evident that religious freedom is a foundation and friend of other freedoms.

THE ORIGINS OF THE HUMAN RIGHTS ETHIC AND ARTICLE 18

In the West, the ethos of human rights grew from Christian natural law traditions, which insisted that governments respect the integrity of human beings, regardless of the will of the ruler. Thus, human rights theories and documents, including those of the United Nations, were not merely imposed by secularists. Nor were they simply the result of a stand-off between the peoples of east and west. Indeed, the very universality of human rights meant that many cultures would come to understand, accept and observe them.

This cross-cultural unity was manifest at the very beginning of the human rights discussions at the United Nations, although the influence of committed Christians was probably strongest. Jacques Maritain, the distinguished French Catholic philosopher, presided over several of the earliest human rights meetings about the Universal Declaration. He sought advice from Greek Orthodoxy, Gandhism, and Confucianism. John Humphrey, who chaired the first drafting committee of the Universal Declaration and was the first Director of the United Nations' Division of Human Rights, said that the Declaration's major proponents included both Catholics and Communists, although the Communists were a distant second. The main political advocates of the

Declaration were Cuba, Chile and Panama (predominantly Christian and Catholic countries at the time). Latin America had produced the 1948 "American Declaration of Human Rights" nine months before the United Nations produced its own Declaration, and the 1948 Bogota "Conference of the American States" provided the framework for the final United Nations version, which was itself produced by Arab, Iranian, Filipino, Chinese, and Indian representatives. The rapporteur of the drafting Commission was Charles Malik, a Lebanese Christian.

Thus, Article 18 was a shared accomplishment: The result of input from a spectrum of religious faiths and a variety of cultures. It could not but be this way for a *Universal* Declaration of Human Rights. Today, most countries accept Article 18, as does nearly every major religious group.

IGNORING RELIGIOUS FREEDOM AS A HUMAN RIGHT

Despite such auspicious beginnings, the United Nations' enforcement of this critical right to religious freedom has been weak, and is getting weaker.

Simply put, the United Nations is reluctant to make religious freedom a priority. Even in the United States, the current campaign against religious persecution is being called "special pleading" and is criticized for creating a "hierarchy of rights" which would downgrade political and racial persecution.[3]

This criticism is strange, and misplaced, since *all* human rights campaigns are "particular pleadings" (that is, they tend to focus on specific causes). Human Rights Watch has special initiatives on drugs and human rights. Amnesty International focuses on prisoners of conscience and the death penalty. When Secretary of State Madeleine Albright announced in 1997 that the United States would pay special attention to the rights of women, there was no complaint. When the State Department Country Reports on Human Rights recently expanded their labor coverage, there was no outcry. When PEN focuses on the defense of writers, it receives no condemnation.

Obviously, protecting a particular human right is not the problem, since all the above champion a particular human right. Do those who oppose such efforts on behalf of the human right to religious freedom deem religious freedom unimportant? Do they think this freedom is not in jeopardy?

If so, they are wrong—on both counts. Religious persecution is massive, growing, and still largely ignored.[4] *New York Times* columnist A.M. Rosenthal recently noted: "Early this year I realized that in decades of reporting, writing or assigning stories on human rights, I rarely touched on one of the most important. Political human rights, legal, civil, and press rights, emphatically often; but the right to worship where and how God or conscience leads, almost never."[5]

WORLD-WIDE RELIGIOUS PERSECUTION

The instances of religious persecution span the globe. In Sudan, the present regime eradicates any non-Islamic expressions or people (and Muslims who disagree) and controls the food supply of refugees dumped in the desert. Non-Muslims are given the choice of converting to Islam or being denied food, clothing and shelter. The unconverted are left to die, naked in the blazing sun. For the converted there is no turning back: Sudan applies the death penalty to anyone who tries to leave Islam.

In China, authorities arrest and sentence underground house-church leaders—often for as long as three years in labor camps. Those who refuse to submit to state control on any matter concerning religion face discrimination, harassment, persecution, and often imprisonment, torture and death. Similar patterns occur in Vietnam, North Korea, and Laos.

Attacks on religious minorities, mostly Christians, have intensified throughout the Islamic belt, from Morocco, on the Atlantic, eastward to the Southern Philippines. While Islam has a tradition of tolerance which continues in some parts of the world, such as Jordan and Kuwait, in many other areas this tolerance has collapsed. In Saudi Arabia, any non-Islamic or dissident Islamic religious expression is forbidden. Any Saudi who seeks to leave Islam faces the real prospect of death. In countries such as Mauritania, the Comorros Islands, and Sudan, this threat is not only from vigilantes, but part of the legal code itself.

In Iran and Pakistan, vigilante groups, with greater or lesser complicity by their governments, are the threat. In Iran there are strong indications that, apart from the persecution of the Baha'i, government death squads have abetted the torture and assassination of Protestant leaders in recent years.

There is violence and discrimination against minority religious groups in non-Islamic societies in Mongolia, Nepal, Sri Lanka, India,

Bhutan and Kampuchea, and in the central Asian republics that were formerly part of the Soviet Union, especially Uzbekistan. It is a growing phenomenon in Burma, where the present regime (SLORC, or the State Law and Order Restoration Campaign) conducts war against tribal minorities, especially the Rohingya Muslims in the west and the Karen and other tribes in the eastern part of the country (where Christians constitute a large proportion of the minorities).

Russia has instituted new, repressive laws on religion with the backing of the Russian Orthodox Church, and there is increasing discrimination, and sometimes violence, against religious minorities, including Jews, Protestants, Catholics and dissident orthodox groups.

Such persecution occurs in dozens of countries, and the above does not even include the more subtle forms of repression and discrimination which occur in dozens more.

WHY RELIGION IS IGNORED

One reason that religious freedom is ignored is that religion itself is also often ignored. When Malaysian Prime Minister Mahathir Mohamed railed against monetary speculators in 1997, stating, "[W]e are Muslims, and the Jews are not happy to see the Muslims progress," the *Los Angeles Times* described him as "race-obsessed."[6] In Yugoslavia, war between Orthodox Christians, Catholics and Muslims is routinely described as "ethnic." *The Economist* ran a story about attacks on 25 churches and a temple in east Java after police reportedly manhandled Muslims. It indexed the story in the table of contents as an article on "race riots."[7]

As Edward Luttwak has noted, "Policy makers, diplomats, journalists, and scholars who are ready to overinterpret economic causality, who are apt to dissect social differentiations ever more finely, and who will minutely categorize political affiliations, are still in the habit of disregarding the role of religion ... in explaining politics and even in reporting their concrete modalities."[8]

Contrary to the implications of media coverage and some of our human rights reporting, the importance of religion the world over is an undeniable fact. To represent the world without this fact in mind is simply to distort reality. The United Nations needs to learn this much, especially given its labors over Article 18. It should consider leading the way in correcting this problem.

"Cultural Context"

Religious repression is also defended by authoritarian governments in the name of "culture." In 1993, China, Vietnam, Indonesia, Iran, Syria, Burma and Singapore produced the "Bangkok Declaration" for the United Nations Vienna Conference on Human Rights. In it, they demanded that human rights be addressed "in the context of national and regional peculiarities and various historical, cultural and religious backgrounds." While no serious commentator doubts that the context for human rights varies from country to country, the Bangkok group went much further and simply rejected any and all criticism of government actions. (Chinese Deputy Foreign Minister Liu Huaqiu inadvertently clarified this by saying: "Nobody should put his rights above those of the state."[9]) Hundreds of millions of other Chinese, such as the underground churches or the students in Tiananmen Square, do not think their persecution is somehow part of Chinese "national culture." Concern for genuine human rights is not some "western culture": It is shared the world over, especially by those whose freedom is denied.

But the mentality of the Bangkok group persists. This was evident at the 1994 Geneva meetings of the U.N. Human Rights Commission. Malaysia, supported by China, Syria, Nigeria, and India, attempted to curtail the powers of the office of the U.N. Special Rapporteur on Religious Intolerance. Sudan then condemned Gaspar Biro, the Special Rapporteur on Sudan, who had reported child slavery, torture, extra-judicial execution, and forced conversion to Islam there.

These attempts to subvert human rights in the name of "culture" must be rejected, if we are serious about protecting the human right to religious freedom. Real respect for cultural differences is, of course, required. No one suggests that this right should not have any limits—one cannot allow human sacrifice in the name of religion. But limits cannot become a pretext for violating fundamental religious liberties.

For example, in the Covenant on Civil and Political Rights (the legal codification of the 1948 Declaration by treaty), religious freedom became subject to "such limitations as are prescribed by law and are necessary to protect public safety, order, health, or morals or the fundamental rights and freedoms of others."[10] Immediately Iran claimed that conversions away from Shiite Islam were "undermining public welfare." Attacks then took place on Sunni Muslims, Christians and Baha'is, with more than 200 of the latter executed since 1979. This cannot continue. In practice, limitations like these become camouflage for gross violations of religious freedom. Indeed, they can be a *carte blanche* to repressive governments.

It is no defense to say that a culture does not value or see religious freedom in the same way as the Declaration. The whole point of recognizing human rights, and a *universal* declaration of human rights no less, is to provide protection for rights that transcend cultural differences, and it is precisely for those in a diversity of cultures that the Universal Declaration exists.

UNITED NATIONS PREOCCUPATION WITH PSEUDO-RIGHTS

A final reason for the erosion of religious freedom is the United Nations' inordinate stress on other "rights," especially what can be called pseudo-rights. For example, the 1995 United Nations Beijing Conference on Women detailed the plight of many women throughout the world, but it ignored their problems of religious persecution and discrimination. (At the last moment, one paragraph on religious liberty was included, having been forgotten in most of the preparatory meetings. Even this, with its point that religion plays "a central role in the lives of millions of women and men," is inaccurate. The correct number is *billions*.) Many in Beijing faulted religious "extremism" for women's problems. The Vatican proposed a statement on religion's positive social effects, but that was dropped. Instead, the Conference focused on and announced new "rights," such as a so-called "right" to abortion and to "control one's sexuality."

It is important to note that these so-called new "rights" have no status in international law. Indeed, many of these new sexual "rights," from abortion to homosexual conduct, are contrary to many valid laws and cultural mores in member nations. Further, this propaganda effort, which has resulted in a proliferation of new, trendy rights, dilutes and undermines real basic human rights such as the right to the freedom of religion. The very term *human rights* tends to be reduced to the latest "progressive" western fad.

As a result of this new focus on so-called "rights," the importance of religious freedom in United Nations circles appears to have waned, and the exercise of this freedom has been seriously curtailed. For example, in the aforementioned Covenant on Civil and Political Rights, there is no longer a right to *change* one's religion, only a right "to *have* or to *adopt* a religion." (This happened largely as a result of pressure by some Arab governments.) This implies that you can join a religion but then there is no right to *change* it. The 1981 Declaration on the Elimination of All Forms of Intolerance and Discrimination Based on Religion or Belief further restricted the language to a right only to *have* a religion [Article 1 (1)].

LOOKING AHEAD

It is perhaps too easy, and maybe unfair, to criticize the United Nations too harshly for its failure to protect religious freedom. After all, it is less an organization with a specific goal than a *forum* where different countries come together to agree, argue or fight. Also, the United Nations machinery for investigating, reporting and censuring something like religious persecution is extremely weak. While many of the United Nations staff are dedicated, they often lack the resources to do anything effective. But the world remains awash in growing religious persecution against Christians, Muslims, Buddhists, Jews, Baha'is, and countless others. And too few are taking note and making efforts to stop it.

We can and should direct such complaints to the United Nations membership. Without support and unity of purpose from its members, the United Nations can and will do little. It can investigate and report violations, to be sure. But, beyond the publicity and embarrassment these reports create for offending nations, the United Nations has few other tools to fight religious oppression.[11] The international agreements it has available are also not especially powerful, since they do not authorize specific remedies for human rights violations.

With care and effort, the United Nations system can become stronger. But this will only happen if its concern for religion is strengthened. If countries do not consider the role of religious faith seriously (and systematically) in human events, then real efforts to protect this human right will shrivel and die, as will the people who cannot count on its protection.

ENDNOTES

[1] This has been the case, for example, in South Africa, Uganda, Kenya, Guatemala, El Salvador, Vietnam, and China.

[2] For example, Turkey, Iraq, Egypt and Indonesia.

[3] See Jacob Heilbrunn, "Christian Rights," *The New Republic* 7 July 1997: 19.

[4] For surveys see: Nina Shea, *In the Lion's Den* (Nashville: Broadman and Holman, 1997); my *Their Blood Cries Out* (Dallas: Word Publishing, 1997); State Department Report, *United States Policies in Support of Religious Freedom: Focus on Christians* (July 1997); State Department Country Reports on Human Rights (1998); and K. Boyle and J. Sheen, *Freedom of Religion and Belief in the World* (London & New York: Routledge, 1997).

[5] A.M. Rosenthal, "A Year of Awakening," *New York Times* 30 Dec. 1997.

[6] Jim Mann, "Malaysia's Economic Woes Turn Up Anti-Semitic Coin," *L.A. Times*, 15 Oct. 1997.

[7] "Indonesia: Signs of Danger," *The Economist*, 4 Jan 1997: 40.

[8] D. Johnston and C. Sampson, eds., "The Missing Dimension," in *Religion: The Missing Dimension of Statecraft* (New York: Oxford University Press, 1994), 9-10.

[9] Liu Paopu and Xiao Qiang, "A Report on the World Conference on Human Rights in Vienna," excerpted from *China Rights Forum*, Fall 1993. This is a remarkable statement, given that the heart of human rights is precisely that some liberties and dignities *are* above the state. See text at 2.

[10] Covenant on Civil and Political Rights, Article 18. Similar language is present in Article 1 of the Declaration of the Elimination of All Forms of Intolerance.

[11] We should not underestimate the effectiveness of this tool, however. Even vicious governments usually try hard to look good.

Chapter 2

The Paramount Human Right: The Right to Life

David Alton

THE HISTORY OF THE HUMAN RIGHTS DECLARATION

Fifty years ago, in the immediate aftermath of the Holocaust and the pre-war slide into eugenics, there was a spirit of determined idealism which helped fashion the United Nations' Declaration of Human Rights. World leaders were deeply affected by the colossal loss of life amongst civilians and the military, but, above all, it was the stench of the concentration camp ovens and the skeleton-like survivors that conditioned post-war thinking.

The 1920s and 1930s had been a period of appeasement and isolationism. Studied indifference greeted the decisions of the German medical and political establishments to promote abortion, euthanasia, the deployment of eugenic techniques and, finally, experiments on human beings. The creation of an Aryan master race, "beautiful people," became an obsessive objective which first took mentally and physically handicapped people, then gypsies, then homosexuals, then Jews and other "non-Aryan" races.

David Alton is a member of Britain's House of Lords.

This was the background against which the United Nations formulated its Declaration. It is not surprising that chief among the human rights enumerated was the very right to life itself. The war's appalling crimes against the person forced the Declaration drafters to spell it out. Article Three states, *"Everyone has the right to life, liberty and security of person."* The drafters were well aware of the failure of pre-war leaders to recognize and protect the internationalist view of human rights, despite the reality that human rights abuses know no customs posts or frontiers. They knew, too, that to avoid the pagan empires of Nazism and Fascism, and the attendant evils of anti-Semitism and xenophobia in the future, the world would need to learn to be its brother's keeper. That is why the United Nations was formed and why it saw the defense of human rights as its central mission.

THE WEST'S OWN HUMAN RIGHTS RECORD: CAUSE FOR CELEBRATION?

Fifty years later, in a year which will be marked by anniversary celebrations, it is worth revisiting the Declaration and questioning whether there is really anything much to celebrate.

Countries such as Britain and the United States consider themselves faithful adherents to human rights policies and supporters of the UN Declaration. Judged against the pledge to defend the right to life, however, such claims look pretty meaningless. It is quite bizarre that many who pride themselves on their belief in human rights do not see the defense of life in the womb as a supreme human rights question—which it undoubtedly is. It is far easier to condemn the human rights abuses in far-away countries (which, of course, must be done) than to confront the transgression of human rights in our own backyard.

In Britain, we have just commemorated 30 years of legal abortion. We have lost more than five million lives, one in every five pregnancies ending in abortion. The United States marks its 25th year of abortion on demand with the anniversary of *Roe v. Wade* in January 1998. Some in each country assert the "right" to destroy the child not just *in utero*, but even in the very process of being born.[1] These anniversaries belie any claim that we are achieving our post-war ideals, or honoring the right to life.

ABORTION: THE HEART OF SOCIETY

Abortion, fundamentally, is about our treatment of the vulnerable and the powerless, a matter that goes to the very heart of a society. Will we consider the unborn, in all their dependency and weakness, to be "persons" and respect them accordingly?

Medical technology, and the ultrasound in particular, has debunked the nonsensical claims of the abortion lobby that the "fetus" is not a person and that abortion merely involves a clump of tissue or a lump of jelly. Now all can plainly see an infant, in all its humanity, before birth. The British Medical Association even recommends that an anesthetic be administered to the child during later abortions, to alleviate the pain of this non-person. Imagine! And still, there is no serious debate about the violation of human rights that the abortion itself constitutes.

The abortion lobby later switched its focus and now emphasizes not just a woman's "*right to choose*," but also her right "*not to be burdened.*" This right is so paramount that it justifies killing. Balancing the rights between mother and child is not an option. Of course, no one likes burdens, so the argument enjoys wide appeal.

In the short space of 30 years, a serious crime has become a right; a public question of law and ethics has become a personal choice; and a practice once firmly repudiated by the medical profession has become a tragic, routine medical procedure—so routine that clinics offer a lunch-box service.

We have regressed to a world where might makes right. The strong simply trample the weak, and we think nothing of it. Indeed, those who fight for the right to life are sidelined as "*single issue*," even though the treatment of the weak is at the heart of who we are. The drafters of the United Nations Declaration knew this only too well. We have forgotten.

ABORTION: THE FAILED PANACEA

Some genuinely believed that abortion would liberate women. Others had a larger agenda, including eugenics testing, genetic engineering, the elimination of disabled people, embryo experimentation, coercive population control, and euthanasia. These are all the old mistakes, really (though Nazi Germany is hardly that old), just presented as "new ideas."

Abortion, of course, has not been the panacea it was promised to be. It has injured more than a generation of women, both psychologically and physically.[2] The incidence of child abuse before and after birth has increased, as has the abuse of women. Men use abortion simply to avoid the responsibilities of fatherhood.

Abortion has fostered an ugly intolerance. Journalists, medical professionals and scientists must support it or suffer professional setbacks. Pro-life students are denied free speech, as are pro-life groups in political parties. Women candidates receive money on the one condition that they support abortion. The British Broadcasting Corporation even allowed a racist General Election broadcast because of the importance of "free speech" while censoring a pro-life one because it might cause offense.

ABORTION: THE DOORWAY TO MORE DESTRUCTION

To what enormities has it all led?

In Great Britain, we now experiment upon or destroy 100,000 human embryos annually. Procedures specifically prohibited on other species by the 1986 Animal Procedures Act are permitted on humans by the 1990 Human Fertilization & Embryology Act.[3] Question abortion and you are reviled as a bigot or a misogynist. In December 1997, 77 of 650 Members of Parliament voted for euthanasia.

THE INTERNATIONAL SCENE

The international scene is no better. China's one-child policy makes it the only country in the world where it is illegal to have a brother or a sister. Its laws now allow the abandonment and killing of disabled newborns. In 1983 alone, the Chinese Population Association oversaw the insertion of 18 million IUDs, 21 million sterilizations, and 14 million abortions. During the same year the U.N. actually rewarded China for controlling its population.

In September 1997, the BBC World Service reported the following:

> "[R]iots have broken out near the southern city of Gozhou after government officials moved in to enforce the country's one-child family planning policy. ... Officials said the trouble began when local residents refused to cooperate with the family planning authorities who were checking whether mothers in the area with one child were sterilized or

fitted with contraceptive devices. Heavy fines are imposed on those who violate China's national policy that allows couples to have only one child."

Great Britain, to the tune of 1 million pounds a year, helps fund all this, as does the United States, where promises to end China's most-favored-nation status appear as hollow as the U.N.'s promises to defend the right to life.

THE INTERNATIONAL PLANNED PARENTHOOD FEDERATION AND THE UNITED NATIONS POPULATION FUND

The money comes to the Chinese Population Association through two major channels: the International Planned Parenthood Federation (IPPF), and the United Nations Population Fund. The IPPF was established in 1952, and in 1983 it made the Chinese Population Association its affiliate, arguing that China should be the model for all nations in population control. IPPF routinely conditions the receipt of international medical and developmental aid on the adoption of the coercive birth control methods outlined above.

IPPF is housed, rent-free, in the offices of the Eugenics Society, whose prominent members include Marie Stopes, who once said that no society "should allow the diseased, the racially negligent, the careless, the feeble-minded, the very lowest and worst members of the community to produce innumerable tens of thousands of warped and inferior infants."[4] Weren't these precisely the attitudes which the writers of the 1948 Declaration of Human Rights believed had so grossly debased pre-war civilization?

GLIMMERS OF HOPE

Ours has been a chaotic century and will be remembered more for its violence and death than for any consistent regard for rights, especially human rights, of which the first is the right to life.

There are hopeful straws in the wind, however. The plaintiff of *Roe v. Wade* now regrets her participation in the case that made abortion on demand legal in the United States. In Great Britain, too, many are revisiting the issue and rejecting an unfettered abortion "right." Citizens are also coming to realize that true protection of the child requires protection of the mother. Women and children are on the same side in this abortion debate because abortion injures and victimizes women. When laws require that we inform a woman of the dangers of abortion for both her life and health as well as the life and health of her child, she may think again, and a life may be saved.

In the larger cultural struggle this next century, we will surely need rather greater courage.

Above all, countries need to return to the themes of 1948 and why we drafted the Universal Declaration on Human Rights in the first place. If ours is going to be a world of common humanity, we need a deep and abiding sense of justice and mercy. We must place human rights at the heart of every foreign and domestic policy. We must recognize that every human being, from conception to natural death, is a creature of body and soul, and is greater than any state.

The sickness which degrades and abuses humanity, and puts the interests of the powerful above those of the weak, has not yet been cured. Genocide, murder, abortion, euthanasia, eugenics, the sale of arms, exploitation and indifference to the poor—all are part of our anti-life, pro-death culture. All represent an abuse of human rights. The relatively powerful exert their lethal dominion over the weak. This is a radical subversion of justice and must be set aright.

None of this will change, and the U.N. Declaration on Human Rights will remain a worthless piece of hollow rhetoric, until national governments and parliaments reassess and re-order their priorities. Governments, in turn, will not change until their citizens have a change of heart. People, you and I, must make human rights as important a question as the level of tax we pay. Landslides happen when small stones start to move. We must be those small stones.

ENDNOTES

[1] David Alton, *Life After Death*, The Christian Democrat Press, Old Hall Green, Ware, Hertfordshire, SG11 1DU, United Kingdom, 1997.

[2] *Ibid.*

[3] Department of Health figures 3. The Rawlinson Report on the effects of abortion on women. CARE, Romney Street, London, 1994.

[4] Marie Stopes, *Radiant Motherhood*, Putnam, 1921.

Chapter 3

Euthanasia and the United Nations' Universal Declaration of Human Rights

Karel Gunning

The United Nations' 1948 Universal Declaration of Human Rights is a remarkable document. It represents the first time in human history that the nations of the world agreed, "Everyone has the right to life, liberty and security of person" (Article 3). While we are far from securing these rights for all, the aim is clear.

Even though all religions agree upon the right to life, the Declaration does not presume a religious foundation, nor does Article 3 rely upon religious faith. Instead, the Declaration's Preamble simply puts the challenge to mankind: If ours is to be a free, just and peaceful world, then we must recognize the inherent dignity and the equal and inalienable rights of all members of the human family. That challenge, it was hoped, would not become dead letter law to forgotten elites. To that end, U.N. member nations were instructed to publicize the Declaration widely, and to post it, especially in schools, so that it would be a continuing inspiration to all citizens.

Karel Gunning is chairman of the World Federation of Doctors Who Respect Human Life in Holland. He led the Dutch Physicians' League as president and then as a board member.

Fifty years later, what has come of this noble Declaration, this expression of world consensus in defense of human rights, chief among them the right to life? Let us look.

Today, many U.N. member states have legalized abortion, the intentional destruction (indeed, the killing) of the child *in utero*, the most vulnerable member of the human family. This is, of course, a gross violation of human rights, specifically the right to life of that child, whose dignity and rights are as inalienable as those of all other living human beings. Have we heard protests from the United Nations General Assembly about this affront to its Universal Declaration? Not a one.

Now, some member countries, or jurisdictions within them, are on the verge of legalizing euthanasia. This too is a direct violation of the Declaration's guarantee of the right to life. Still no word from the U.N.

THE HISTORICAL CONTEXT

We would do well to return to 1948, the year the Declaration was drafted, or earlier, to understand how this document came into being and why it was ever deemed needed.

Nineteen forty-eight was the aftermath of the second World War. Almost all Europe had been ravaged. The loss of life was inconceivable. But the loss of life did not begin on the battlefields or in the shipping lanes. It did not begin with the clash of armies or the acts of saboteurs. It began in the halls of medicine. It began with deeds of "mercy," or euthanasia. During World War II, more than 100,000 German patients were euthanized. Those killings solved the "problem" of unwanted patients in Nazi Germany. The problem of "unwanteds" in other areas (politics, social life, etc.) was also solved by killing.

That is how it goes when killing becomes the solution: If today we accept the intentional killing of a patient as a solution for one problem, then tomorrow we will find a hundred problems for which killing will also be accepted as a solution.

This brutal and cavalier destruction of human life during the second World War prompted the nations of the world to conceive of a document that would protect human beings from similar violations in the future. The Declaration, by making human rights explicit, and by making their protection a universal goal, is that document.

OUR LOST HUMANITARIAN ETHIC

In 1948, the world's leading nations, and all U.N. members, agreed on the content of human rights. We shared an ethic that the Declaration, and Article 3 in particular, expresses. I call this the humanitarian ethic. It also informs the Hippocratic oath which, of course, is pre-Christian (400 BC). In this ethic, the sanctity of the person and the true well-being of the patient are central: No one can assign the patient value because he has inherent worth. Hippocrates recognized, however, that doctors could easily violate this ethic since they, by training, have the power not just to cure but also to kill. It was for this reason that Hippocrates made doctors swear that they would never use their knowledge and experience to kill, not even at a patient's own request. The oath enabled medicine to protect the vulnerable patient, no matter how sick, and enabled society to preserve the sanctity of the human person, no matter how weak.

We share no such ethic today. Indeed, we seem in the process of discarding the humanitarian ethic to embrace a utilitarian one. The utilitarian ethic does not care about the individual patient; it cares about the interests of the many. In such a system, the doctor must decide whether the patient is a benefit or a burden to others. The question is no longer, "What is best for this patient?" but, "What is most useful to society?"

Society often sells this ethic as an advance in autonomy for the patient. In fact, it is simply increased power for doctors. As Hippocrates anticipated, physicians decide who lives and who dies.

Anyone in doubt about this prospect should read the September 1970 editorial of *California Medicine*.[1] It recognized that the dominant ethic in Western medicine had been the humanitarian one, where every life was deemed of equal worth. This simply could not continue, the editorial noted, in a world where overpopulation was so serious a threat. It concluded that we cannot continue to accept just any life of any quality. Instead, each life should be assigned a value, and choices made accordingly. The editorial did not call for intentional killing (since vestiges of the old ethic still rendered "killing" socially abhorrent); it simply predicted "death control" and death selection, just as we have birth control and birth selection. And doctors needed to prepare for the new era and its new tasks.

Can anyone doubt that respect for all human life diminishes, and violence against the weak increases with such an "ethic"? Indeed, in such a world euthanasia becomes a duty.

There is no need even to speculate on this point. We have the perfect case study right now. It is my country, Holland.

THE NETHERLANDS

The first few landmark cases of euthanasia in the Netherlands in the 1970s were supposedly voluntary (involving a patient's request for death) and only in extreme circumstances where a patient was near the end of life or in uncontrollable and unbearable physical pain. Today, there is no end to the category of patients who can be euthanized.

Newborn babies with disabilities are at very, very high risk. Premature infants, or those with spina bifida or Down's Syndrome, are often candidates for death by starvation and dehydration.[2] They are often denied life saving medical treatment, even relatively simple kinds, just because of their disabilities and the presumption that they will have "unlivable" lives.[3] Some are given lethal injections.[4]

A similar risk exists for the mentally ill. One family found their Alzheimer's patient comatose after one week in a nursing home. He had been deliberately dehydrated. The family took him immediately to a hospital where he was given fluids intravenously. Today, months later, he is still alive.[5]

Even completely healthy but depressed people are not safe. Doctors in favor of euthanasia appear always ready to recommend or grant a request for death, even if the patient is despondent.[6] Are we to believe that all these are voluntary deaths? A newborn cannot offer consent to anything, much less to its own killing. Nor should the law withdraw protection for the mentally ill, whose power to give consent is attenuated in myriad ways, and for whom the temptation to accept euthanasia may be just one more symptom of their illness.

We do have figures for the number of cases of euthanasia in the Netherlands. But the Dutch Government considers a case "euthanasia" only if a patient's request is involved. Those cases where a patient dies without any request (or consent) at all are not included in this limited definition.[7] By contrast, the internationally accepted definition of *euthanasia* includes these cases (as it should). For this reason, the numbers of the Dutch government can be misleading.

For example, the famous Remmelink report, issued by a government-installed committee headed by the former Dutch Attorney General, surveyed the practice of euthanasia in Holland for the year 1990.[8]

There was another such report in 1995.[9] For 1995, the Dutch government claimed that euthanasia (by its definition) had been applied in "only" 2.4 percent of all deaths (this would be a 30 percent increase from 1990, where it found that euthanasia accounted for 1.8 percent of all deaths). But by international standards, euthanasia constituted almost 20 percent of all deaths in the Netherlands because the international definition includes cases of assisted suicide (0.3 percent), administration of lethal drugs without the consent of the patient (0.7 percent), intensified pain relief with at least partial intent to hasten death (2.9 percent), and non-treatment decisions with the explicit intention of hastening death (13.3 percent). For 1995, there were almost 26,600 cases of euthanasia (as defined internationally), of which only 13,300 were at the patient's request.

A change in Dutch law makes it possible today for a doctor to end a patient's life without being prosecuted, provided the doctor follows written "guidelines," such as obtaining a second opinion (though not necessarily from mental health experts or palliative care specialists), completing a questionnaire, and the like. But the euthanizing doctor remains in control of the information, and the prosecutor acts, or does not act, depending on this information. The chief witness (the patient) is, of course, dead.

In brief, the new law protects doctors who kill their patients, not patients who are killed by doctors.

Worse still, the utilitarian, pro-death mentality is now the norm in Dutch medicine. An internist friend once told me that he needed a lung cancer patient hospitalized. He assured this patient that she would not be euthanized there. He admitted her himself, and within 36 hours her breathing was easier and her overall condition better. When the internist was off duty, however, a colleague euthanized her. His justification: "We need that bed for another case. It makes no difference for her whether she dies today or after a fortnight."[10]

Indeed, upon hearing of British successes with palliative care, some Dutch doctors claim that they do not need it since they have euthanasia![11]

Dutch society now expects physicians to practice euthanasia for their convenience.

A colleague of mine once recalled a case of an old man who was to die any day. His son had planned a holiday and wanted the funeral to occur before he left. So this colleague gave the old man a huge dose of morphine, expecting it to kill him. He was amazed to discover later that the patient was sitting happily on the edge of his bed. At last he had been given enough morphine to kill his pain! But this colleague told the story as if it were the most normal thing to do, to kill a patient to suit his family's schedule.[12]

THE CHALLENGE

It is tragic and frightening that Holland has embraced death as a solution to medical and social problems. It did not and does not have to be this way. Other nations have not abandoned their sick as we have. In Great Britain, there is "palliative care" which treats not only the physical symptoms of terminal disease, but the loneliness, the fear, and the suffering that come with dying. Instead of killing patients, they alleviate their pain.

The World Health Organization (WHO) has done magnificent work in combating infectious disease in the world. Now euthanasia threatens to kill even more people. What will we do to combat this new aggressor? We can make palliative or hospice care available to every patient in the world who needs it. We can begin an educational campaign so that not only doctors, but patients and families too, know that modern medicine can relieve even the most intense pain, with adequate drug doses. We can promise to stand by our patients, in keeping with our humanitarian ethic, and not dispose of them as useless commodities in a cold utilitarian system.

This is the challenge to medicine today and to the United Nations. The challenge tests our faithfulness to our humanitarian tradition, expressed so well in the Universal Declaration of Human Rights. Will we uphold this tradition, and restore the first human right, the right to life? Or will we adopt a utilitarian ethic, where death is deemed a solution and the sick, the weak, and the needy are simply eliminated?

I, for one, favor the original promise of the Declaration. I hope this fiftieth anniversary reminds us to honor it.

ENDNOTES

[1] "A New Ethic for Medicine and Society." *Official Journal of the California Medical Association* 113 (1970): 67-68.

[2] Fenigsen, Richard, M.D., Ph.D. "Dutch Euthanasia Revisited." *Issues in Law & Medicine* 13 (1997): 301. *See also* "Infants' Euthanasia Sets Off New Dutch Debate." *American Medical News* 1 Jan 1996; and Fenigsen. "Physician-Assisted Death in the Netherlands: Impact on Long-Term Care." *Issues in Law & Medicine* 11 (1995): 283, 294-295.

[3] Fenigsen, *supra* note 2.

[4] *Id.*

[5] *NRC-HANDELSBLAD* [Rotterdam] 25 July 1997.

[6] For example, a psychiatrist who had helped a depressed but healthy woman commit suicide was acquitted. *"Psychiater Vrijuit Na Hulp bij Zelfdoding,"* [Psychiatrist Goes Free after Help with Suicide] *Algermeen Dagblad* [Rotterdam] 22 April 1993.

[7] Borst-Eilers, E. "Euthanasia in the Netherlands: Brief Historical Review and Present Situation." *Euthanasia: The Good of the Patient, The Good of Society.* Ed. R.I. Misbin. Frederick, Maryland: University Publishing Group, 1992. This was true also for newborns who had their own category in the 1991 Remmelink report.

[8] van der Maas, P.J. and J.J.M. van Delden, *et al. Medische Beslissingen Rond Het Levenseinde*, SDU den Haag 1991.

[9] van der Wal, G. and P.J. van der Maas, *Euthanasie en andere medische beslissingern rond het Levenseinde,* SDU, den Haag 1996.

[10] Personal communication with author.

[11] van der Does de Villebois, J.A. *"Waarom dit westonwerp niet?"* (Why Not this Bill?) in *Vita Humana* (Official Paper of the Dutch Physicians' League), April 1989: 1.

[12] Personal communication with author.

Chapter 4

The "Right to Health" According to WHO

Isabel Bilmore

Nineteen-ninety eight is the fiftieth anniversary of both the United Nations' Universal Declaration of Human Rights and the United Nations' World Health Organization (WHO), the agency responsible for international health standards. WHO's new ethic, to be adopted at the World IIcalth Assembly in May of 1998, will emphasize more than ever the "right to health," even though this "right" appears in neither the Universal Declaration nor WHO's own constitution. In fact, WHO's interpretation of this new right would take us further away than we already are from the Universal Declaration's vision of human dignity.

This essay will explain WHO's "right to health" and its implications for the goals of the Universal Declaration and for our culture.

THE "RIGHTS APPROACH" OF THE 1990S

Never has the United Nations (U.N.) spoken more of human rights

Isabel Bilmore is a journalist and writer based in Europe. In the last five years, she has produced numerous studies and articles on international organizations for European publications.

than in recent years. The "rights approach," as this trend is called in U.N. documents, is fueled by the seemingly endless creation of "new rights," the philosophy of which is often incompatible with the Universal Declaration.

These new rights are all part of the U.N.'s new anthropological vision for the post Cold War age.[1] This vision is called, rather euphemistically, "sustainable development." Sustainable development has been defined as a balance system between economic growth, social equity, and environmental protection.[2] It is actually a campaign for the reign of hedonistic individualism with no room for traditional values or for true human rights.

The U.N. speaks of the coming century as one of "human rights, peace and democracy," but it fails to disclose how it is reinterpreting "human rights" in a way that fundamentally threatens the dignity of human beings. An examination of WHO's new "right to health" provides an example of this present UN thinking.

THE WHO "RIGHT TO HEALTH"

What is this new "right to health"? Is it a human right, found in the Universal Declaration? Does it foster respect for the "inherent dignity ... of all members of the human family" as the Declaration prescribes?[3]

Article 25 of the Universal Declaration states, "Everyone has the right to a standard of living adequate for the health and well-being of himself and of his family, including ... medical care."[4] The WHO constitution declares, "The enjoyment of the highest attainable standard of health is one of the fundamental rights of every human being."[5] Neither of these, however, is a "right to health" as such, much less the "right to health" envisioned by WHO.[6] Yet, since 1978, WHO has spoken of a "fundamental human right" to health as if it were a written part of both texts.[7]

How does WHO interpret this "fundamental human right" to health?

WHO defines "health" as "a state of total physical, social and mental well-being, not merely the absence of disease or infirmity."[8] This, of course, equates "health" with "well-being." (By contrast, the Universal Declaration recognizes the two as distinct: It speaks of health *and* well-being.) In May 1998, governments from around the world will vote on whether to add "spiritual well-being" to this list.

This pretense is quite dangerous in our individualistic culture: A right to health, as defined above, can conveniently justify simply doing what you want, since doing otherwise risks upsetting your emotional (or mental, or spiritual) "well-being." Abortion would be the archetypal example. If a woman has a "right to total well-being," she can easily justify an abortion pursuant to her "right to health," since the pregnancy may upset her and be a hindrance to her total well-being.[9] In this way, WHO violates the Declaration's explicit guarantee to the right to life,[10] in the name of a new and ever-changing "right to health."

THE "HEALTH FOR ALL" STRATEGY

WHO adopted a strategy titled "Health for All" in 1978. The implications of this campaign are equally troubling.

"Health for All" is essentially the adoption of primary health care as an absolute priority in WHO policy and practice. Primary health care is mostly preventive care for healthy people. It is defined as an approach to health that embodies universal coverage (hence "health for all") in relation to need and resources. In fact, it is a system where WHO determines others' "needs" according to its own priorities and resources. These priorities are usually ideological and often include abortion, contraception, and health "education," instead of real medical services.[11]

In sum, where primary health care is most important, those most in need of medical attention (the sick) can be neglected.[12] The supposed appeal of such a system is the promise of universal access and the so-called "principle of equity."[13] But this principle, in practice, becomes subject to arbitrary decision-making on the part of WHO based on economics, not medical need.

THE REPLACEMENT OF "LIFE EXPECTANCY" WITH "HEALTH EXPECTANCY" AND THE ABANDONMENT OF THE SICK

WHO appears to define "health" as others might define "quality of life": that is, the presence of comfort, ease, and pleasure in one's day to day living. For WHO, however, this concept becomes the essence and meaning of life. From this perspective, when a life lacks "quality," it lacks meaning. In this scheme, suffering has no value and must be exterminated at all moral and other costs.

The 1997 WHO annual report states explicitly that life expectancy has less value than the new concept of "health expectancy." Dr. Hiroshi Nakajima, WHO's present Director General, wrote:

[W]hile congratulating ourselves on these extra years that prolong our lives, we must recognize that without quality of life, longer life is uninteresting and that health expectancy is more important than life expectancy.[14]

The idea here is clearly that those who are unhealthy and thus unable to enjoy a certain "quality of life," have lives that are not "worth living." This mentality is frighteningly reminiscent of crass philosophies about the value of certain human beings (the mentally ill and others) popular in Europe before the second World War.[15] It is a great affront to the "right to life" guaranteed by the Universal Declaration and it inevitably promotes euthanasia: When your "health expectancy" is over, why should you still live? WHO's reinterpretation of human rights to include a right to "health" and "health expectancy" can lead us nowhere else.

The immediate and practical effect of substituting "health expectancy" for life expectancy is the neglect of those whose "quality of life" does not or cannot meet some arbitrary WHO health standard. As Nakajima put it:

It appears absurd to see a child survive polio one year if he is going to die of malaria the following year, or will not grow healthy to become a productive adult.[16]

By this standard, of course, medical treatment for the very sick is an absurdity, since they, almost by definition, cannot even hope to become "productive adults," as Nakajima puts it. Thus, neither the "right to health" nor the "Health for All" campaign will extend to the terminally ill, the handicapped, the unborn and the truly sick. They have no place in WHO's health care programs. Indeed, by adopting such priorities, WHO has effectively abandoned those who need care the most, the weak and the sick.

REPRODUCTIVE AND SEXUAL RIGHTS

Since the 1994 U.N. Population Conference in Cairo, the new WHO "right to health" has emphasized "reproductive rights" (that is, contraception, abortion, AIDS prevention, and sex education for teenagers) so much that it has, in some instances, seemed to concern them almost exclusively. For example, WHO presented a "school-health initiative" as part of a "health education" program in schools, that was, in reality, almost all AIDS prevention instruction.[17]

The introduction of such subversive concepts as "reproductive health" and "reproductive rights" was the real breakthrough at Cairo. "Reproductive health" is defined as "a state of complete physical, mental and social well-being ... in all matters relating to the reproductive system and to its function and processes."[18] Although many governments expressed reservations about these concepts, the Cairo documents were said to enjoy worldwide consensus. This consensus now serves as justification for imposing (or "mainstreaming," in U.N.-speak) so-called "reproductive rights" throughout the member nations of the U.N. and U.N. agencies.

WHO and the United Nations Population Fund (UNFPA) have since boasted about the "people-centered approach" used to promote these concepts, contrasting it with past "top-down" coercive population control methods.[19] The new approach, they bragged, stresses the need to make people (teenagers in particular) aware of their "needs and rights" in the area of sexuality through sensitization campaigns.

WHO appears completely oblivious to the conflict such propaganda campaigns pose with the Universal Declaration. Insofar as they promote abortion, they most certainly offend the Universal Declaration's guarantee of the right to life in Article Three.[20] In addition, they violate Articles 18 and 26(3), which protect a parent's "prior right to choose the kind of education that shall be given to their children" and everyone's "right to freedom of thought, conscience and religion."[21] It should also be noted that the very concept of "reproductive health" is incompatible with major world religions, as is the "sexual rights" movement (advocating absolute sexual license), which includes the acceptance of homosexuality, all of which WHO encourages. Traditional religions, of course, have always stressed the human person as a self-giving entity. By contrast, WHO and its myriad "rights" envision and encourage the human person to be a selfish individual whose sexual satisfaction seemingly comes before all else.

CONCLUSION: NEW ETHIC

The WHO "right to health" and "Health for All" campaigns are part of an ever-evolving new ethic that does not recognize the inherent dignity of each human being and therefore cannot observe real human rights. In such a world, the sick do not warrant medical care, the weak perish through euthanasia, and the unborn die by abortion, while the insatiable, sexual self reigns supreme. In the end, WHO's renewed emphasis on the "right to health" is an assault upon human dignity and a violation of our Universal Declaration.

During this fiftieth anniversary of the Universal Declaration of Human Rights, we might ask whether we really want this new ethic, and, if not, what we might do to restore the old one.

ENDNOTES

[1] These rights generally include "reproductive rights" (contraception and abortion and the propaganda to promote them), environmental rights, sexual rights, the rights of public health, the right to development, the right to housing, women's rights, and children's rights.

[2] Brundtland, Gro Harlem, *Our Common Future*, United Nations Report (1987). Ms. Brundtland will soon become WHO's new Director General. The "social equity" component of this definition includes "reproductive" and "sexual" rights (that is, abortion and contraception and promotional "awareness campaigns" for the same).

[3] United Nations, *Universal Declaration of Human Rights* (1948), Preamble, Par. 1.

[4] *Id.* Article 25.

[5] United Nations, World Health Organization Constitution, Preamble.

[6] The right to a standard of living is not the same as a "right to health"; nor is enjoyment of the highest reachable standard of health a "right to health."

[7] WHO Conference on Primary Health Care at Alma Ata.

[8] *Supra* note 5.

[9] The head of the WHO Division on Reproductive Health, Dr. Tomris Turmen, provided the Cairo definition of these rights (1994 Conference on Population and Development). She established the following hierarchy in her programs: the woman first, then the mother, then the newborn baby, then the child. In the name of women's rights, the woman comes first. Thus can abortion almost always be justified.

[10] *Supra* note 3, Article 3.

[11] Indeed, primary health care focuses on nutrition, safe water and sanitation, literacy, and vaccination campaigns, not medical treatment for the sick.

[12] This is especially true if the sick are unlikely to become productive individuals. See *infra* note 16 and accompanying text.

[13] WHO (position paper), *Health in Social Development*, World Summit for Social Development (1995). (Equity "represents the principle of universality in health promotion and care, with the aim that all human beings may live free

from the risk of preventable illness and injury and may have equal access to quality health care that is both affordable and relevant.")

[14] United Nations World Health Organization Annual Report, 1997.

[15] Michael Burleigh, *Death and Deliverance: "Euthanasia" in Germany c. 1900-1945* (New York: Cambridge University Press, 1994), discussing Binding & Hoche pamphlet.

[16] The World Health Assembly. Speech. 1991.

[17] The Health Education and Health Promotion Units of WHO promote these school initiatives.

[18] The United Nations, *Achieving Reproductive Health for All: The Role of WHO* (1995) at 3.

[19] In the past, the U.S. Government and WHO imposed population control projects on governments of developing countries. The top-down imposition was reflected in the expression "population control," which has almost disappeared from current U.N. language. Now, "reproductive health" is said to be a need expressed by the people themselves, and is presented as a "bottoms-up" program. National Security Council Report (the Kissinger Report), *Implications of Worldwide Population Growth for US Security and Overseas Interests*, 1974.

[20] WHO's most recent technical report on "Medical Methods for Termination of Pregnancy" demonstrates that WHO considers safe abortion an integral part of reproductive health. It reads: "Unsafe abortion is a worldwide public health problem of considerable magnitude that can be solved only by better provision of contraception and safe abortion procedures. Consequently, the Special Program has supported research on the health consequences and the prevention of abortion as well as on the safety and effectiveness of the various methods employed for inducing abortion." WHO Technical Report Series 871, *Medical Methods for Termination of Pregnancy* (1997) at 1. Nafis Sadik, the Executive Director of the United Nations Population Fund (UNFPA) who collaborates closely with the WHO Reproductive Health Division, recently declared her intention to ensure that reproductive rights are integrated into the human rights treaty monitoring process, so that governments are legally bound to implement her agenda: "UNFPA strongly supports the proposal that CEDAW make a general recommendation elaborating on Article 12 of the Convention to spell out countries' obligations with regard to women's health, including their sexual and reproductive health." Dr. Nafis Sadik, Statement to The Committee on the Elimination of Discrimination Against Women, New York, 30 Jan. 1998.

[21] *Supra* note 3, Articles 18 & 26(3).

Chapter 5

Is Cloning Compatible with Human Rights and Human Dignity?

Henk Jochemsen

We reached a scientific milestone on July 5, 1996, with the birth of Dolly, the sheep.[1] Dolly is a clone. For the first time, science had proved that it could make a clone from a mature higher mammal.

The possibility this event raises of applying cloning techniques to produce human clones has enormous implications for the individual and for society. This paper addresses those concerns from a human rights perspective informed by the Universal Declaration of Human Rights, as well as other international documents and philosophies.

CLONING: WHAT IS IT?

Cloning means creating genetically identical individuals. Genetic material is within the nucleus of any cell (except for some blood cells). The cloning of Dolly involved removing the nucleus from a grown sheep's udder cell and then placing that nucleus into a sheep egg cell

Henk Jochemsen, Ph.D., is director of the Prof. Dr. G.A. Lindeboom Institute, Centre for Medical Ethics in Ede, and holder of the Lindeboom chair for medical ethics in Amsterdam, The Netherlands.

(or ovum) whose own nucleus had been removed. The resulting egg cell, containing the nucleus from the donor sheep, was then stimulated to behave as a fertilized egg cell, or a zygote. It then began embryonic development. Shortly thereafter, scientists transferred this embryo to the uterus of an adult sheep. This led to the birth of a healthy lamb, Dolly.

Dolly is genetically identical (with insignificant exceptions) to the sheep that provided the nucleus of the udder cell, or the nuclear donor sheep.[2] Dolly can be considered a monozygotic twin of that donor sheep, brought about by means of a biotechnological intervention.

The successful use of this cloning technique implies that we could create embryos artificially from every mammalian cell, including human cells, and develop them into new individuals, each of whom would be genetically identical to the donor of the cell from which the nucleus was taken.

Two biological facts are most noteworthy about the resulting clone. Whereas the typical fertilized egg cell occurring in nature gets its genetic material from both a male and a female parent, the clone gets its genetic material from a single donor (the donor of the nucleus). Further, normal fertilization creates a new and *unique* combination of the genes of the two parents, resulting in a genetically unique individual. By contrast, the cloned individual has the exact gene pattern of the individual from which the nucleus was taken. The clone's genetic composition is *not* unique.

FOR WHAT WOULD CLONING BE USED?

Advocates of human cloning propose a number of possible uses for the production of human clones.

ARTIFICIAL PROCREATION. The first and most obvious area of interest is artificial procreation. Infertile couples could produce a clone of one parent as an alternative to the traditional means of having a child. (From a strictly genetic point of view, however, the child would be a monozygotic twin of the cloned parent.) Homosexual couples could also make use of cloning to reproduce. Finally, some parents might want to store tissues of their children to have the option of cloning a child who might die prematurely.[3]

Cloning humans might also lead to reproducing people with desired characteristics, the idea being, of course, that the clone, having the same gene pattern as the "original," would also have the same desirable characteristics. Accomplishing this is not at all certain, however, since human traits are always formed under the influence of environmental factors as well as genetic ones. Mark McGwire's clone, without hours of baseball training, would be no Mark McGwire.

BIOMEDICAL APPLICATIONS. Researchers claim that human cloning would advance certain areas of biomedicine. Shortly after the news of Dolly broke, national and international ethics committees began to talk about a distinction between reproductive and non-reproductive cloning.[4] The former implies the birth of a human individual genetically identical to an already existing human being. The latter would involve letting a clone develop until the embryonic stage without transferring the embryo to the uterus of a woman. Instead, the embryo would be kept in a petri dish for future medical use.[5]

The use of non-reproductive cloning as a basic biotechnological procedure could have at least the following three applications:

1. CULTURING TISSUES AND ORGANS OF PATIENTS WHO SUFFER FROM A DEFICIENCY IN THE FUNCTIONING OF THOSE TISSUES OR ORGANS

Scientists can create tissue that is genetically compatible with a patient by taking the nucleus from any of the patient's cells and creating a clone embryo. They maintain the embryo in a culture in a petri dish. From the central part of this embryo (the so-called *inner cell mass*), they then produce a culture of embryonic stem cells (ES cells). This is a very recent development for scientists.[6] Then they can induce a sample of that culture to develop into specific kinds of cells and tissues, such as brain tissue, pancreas tissue, and so on. That cultured tissue can be transplanted into the patient from whom the nucleus was removed. There is no risk of the patient's immune system rejecting the tissue, because, of course, it is genetically identical to his own tissue.

2. EXTENSIVE GENETIC SELECTION OF EMBRYOS *IN VITRO*

Right now it is already possible to screen embryos for the presence of one or two genetic disorders. This process is called *pre-implantation genetic diagnosis*. It involves removing one or two cells from the embryo for examination and diagnostic testing.

The combination of cloning by nuclear transfer and the culturing of embryonic stem cells will make it possible to screen more embryos for a larger number of possible genetic defects. Scientists can simply create embryonic stem cell cultures from the embryos targeted for screening. The cell cultures allow for more extensive investigation of genetic baggage from the targeted embryo. Obviously, only those embryos with the most favorable genetic constitution will be selected for implantation within the mother to make the journey to birth.

3. GENETIC MODIFICATION OF THE GERM LINE

Genetic modification of the germ line means altering the genes of human beings and their progeny. At the moment, this practice is too risky to attempt to perform on human beings. But a few biomanipulations could reduce the risk sufficiently in the future that scientists will feel comfortable trying it.

If a scientist wished to modify the genetic composition of a human being's progeny, the scientist would create an embryonic clone of that person and then create a culture with embryonic stem cells of that human embryo. The culture would be modified in the petri dish. The scientist then would remove the nucleus of the successfully modified cell and use this nucleus to create a new embryo (a clone of the original embryo but with the modification). That embryo could then be transferred to the womb to develop to birth.

All this could be made possible by both nuclear transfer cloning and more and more sophisticated culturing of embryonic stem cells.

Given the potential for improvements in certain types of medical treatment, many have said that such non-reproductive cloning should be allowed (since this does not necessarily result in the birth of a clone of an already existing person). When politicians and other representatives of the public called for a ban on human cloning, scientists cautioned them to exclude non-reproductive human cloning research from any such ban.[7] So-called "non-reproductive cloning" does involve, however, the manipulation and loss of human embryos *in vitro*, since they are "forced" to develop into embryonic stem cell cultures.

WHAT OBJECTIONS CAN BE RAISED?

Several dimensions of cloning invoke human rights objections and should give us pause. Some of the more noteworthy follow.

1. MEDICAL RISKS TO THE CLONE

It is important to realize that most sheep embryos brought about by cloning died soon after being created (during gestation or soon after birth) due to congenital disorders. Dolly was the only healthy lamb born from 277 embryos created by nuclear transfer.[8] In one case, a lamb was about twice the normal size and could be born only by cesarean section. (The same phenomenon has been observed in the cloning of cows.) In one experiment with mice, only 17 live fetuses made it to birth from 800 embryos, and only 10 of those 17 survived to raise healthy offspring. A first generation of cloned human beings would be subjected to these and other unforeseeable risks—not only at the embryonic stage, but also after birth.

All this is clearly unfair to the cloned individual and would violate Article 3 of the Universal Declaration of Human Rights (UDHR), which states: "Everyone has the right to life, liberty and **security of person**" (emphasis added). It is also at odds with provisions of other U.N. documents, such as Article 6.2 of the Convention on the Rights of the Child (CRC), which states: "States parties shall ensure, to the maximum extent possible, the survival and development of the child."

2. OTHER RISKS TO THE CLONE

Biological and medical risks to the clone are not the only concern. There are psychological and social risks as well.

Producing a child of known genetic constitution implies conditional acceptance, which is detrimental for any child's development. Research indicates that unconditional acceptance by parents is favorable to positive psychological development of a child.[9]

Cloning even deprives the cloned child of his natural parents, for he does not have parents in the usual sense of the word. From a genetic point of view, the biological parents of the clone are the parents of the nuclear donor—and the clone's sociological grandparents. These changed relations will have an emotional and therefore developmental impact on the clone.

Then there is the case of the ovum donor and the woman who bears the child and gives birth. This can be, but need not be, the same woman. It is possible that one woman could provide all three elements: the nucleus, the ovum and the uterus. That woman would in a sense give birth to her own monozygotic twin.

Thus, human cloning will clearly disturb family relationships in a serious way. It is hard to justify such large-scale disruption (both at the familial and societal level) for the rare case when parents wish to reproduce a child who has died at a young age. (And even in such cases—in fact, especially in such cases—we still face the problems of manufacturing children and treating them as products.) Confusion regarding family relationships is not good for children, who benefit from stable families.

The United Nation's Convention on the Rights of the Child clearly states: "The child shall have the right from birth to a name ... and as far as possible, the right to know and be cared for by his or her parents." It goes on: "States parties undertake to respect the right of the child to preserve his or her identity ... name and family relations as recognized by law without unlawful interference." Cloning, of course, confounds such declarations, since it upsets the standard parent-child structure.

3. LOSS OF EMBRYOS

Human cloning almost necessarily means the loss of intentionally created human embryos, given the techniques and applications mentioned above. There has been considerable discussion about the status of the human embryo, both within the field of bioethics and in society at large, especially in the context of the abortion issue.

With respect to abortion, though, the killing of the unborn child is supposedly justified because of the woman's interests (for example, a right to self-determination), which are said to be in conflict with those of the child. Quite apart from the question of whether these interests justify abortion, it is clear that in the context of cloning there is no such conflict. No right to "self-determination" or to "control one's own body" is at stake. Instead, scientists would intentionally create human embryos, and then kill them, to fulfill certain demands.

The desire to have one's own children, as well as the desire to have healthy children, is understandable. But such desires cannot justify using human embryos as if they were simply a biological means to a desired end.

Human embryos undeniably belong to the human family. This is a matter of biological fact. According to the Universal Declaration's Preamble, then, our recognition of their inherent dignity, and of their equal and inalienable rights, is the foundation of freedom, justice and peace in the world.[10] The Preamble of the Convention on the Rights of the Child also says as much: "[T]he child ... needs special safeguards and care, including appropriate legal protection before as well as after birth."[11]

The European Parliament's March 12, 1997, Resolution on *Cloning Animals and Human Beings* also rejects cloning in the context of embryo research. Article 3 "urges member states to ban the cloning of human beings at all stages of formation and development, regardless of the method used. ..."[12]

4. HUMAN CLONING AS CONTRARY TO HUMAN RIGHTS AND DIGNITY

Jewish scholar Abraham Heschel provides insight and context for the human cloning discussion, offering a framework within which to interpret international declarations or other documents on the question. Heschel distinguishes two fundamentally different ways in which the human being can relate to reality: *manipulation* and *appreciation*. With the former, the individual views his surroundings as things to handle, to control, and to utilize. With the latter, the individual views his surroundings as things to accept, to comprehend, to appreciate or to admire.[13]

Manipulation, Heschel contends, is the cause of alienation, for there is no bond between the individual and his surroundings except utility. Ultimately, the individual is alone and things have no meaning apart from his use for them.

In our modern age, especially in scientific and technological areas, the attitude of manipulation dominates. In fact, the pro-technology mentality encourages this approach to reality, for technology is now the chief instrument to control and manipulate the environment. Manipulators of technology begin to see reality itself only in terms of utility and meaning *for them*. For them, nothing has meaning in and of itself.   The individual becomes the only source of meaning for all things, and, especially worrisome, for all other individuals.   This mentality signals the death of transcendence, particularly the transcendence of man.

This approach to reality distorts life. The modern age itself is evidence of this. So many people in our time feel that their lives have no real meaning—because they do not realize that true meaning is not something we generate. It is, rather, given to us. We have only to acknowledge and accept it.

Human beings have a dimension of transcendence, as does the creation of new human beings. We are not just the ordered conglomerate of cells. Each person is a mystery, not just a predictable product of parents. Parents in particular know this as they discover that they cannot completely understand or explain their own children on the basis of who they are themselves.[14] In each child there is something new and unique, something that ultimately remains beyond our control. This is as it should be.

Cloning is an attempt to bring that mystery under our control. It would reduce the child (at least in his or her biological constitution) to "a carbon copy" of one of his or her parents. This cannot fully succeed, of course, since the cloned child would be a unique human being (as well as influenced by necessarily different environmental factors). But that kind of reproduction itself changes the parent-child relationship. The clone is the projection of somebody else. His biological characteristics were programmed.

Through cloning, a process of creation becomes a process of manufacturing. A child becomes a product. And a product is never considered equal to its producer. The child's own character is compromised, as he is no longer received as a transcendent gift. The claim that the cloned child will be accepted and loved for who he is overlooks both the structural change in the parent-child relationship and this compromise of transcendence.

The human being's unique genetic constitution is the biological foundation of his moral freedom and independence. It is also, therefore, fundamental to his dignity and his equality to all human beings. If one human being becomes, even to a very small extent, the product of intentional technological manipulations of others, all this is undermined. We tamper with this foundation at the risk of human rights.

It is for this reason that cloning and enhanced genetic modification (aimed at improving human beings and their progeny) contradict Article 1 of the Universal Declaration on Human Rights, which states, "All human beings are born free and equal in dignity and rights." The Universal Declaration on the Human Genome and Human Rights (accepted by the General Conference of UNESCO, d.d. 11-11-1997A) is more straightforward: "Practices which are contrary to human dignity, such as reproductive cloning of human beings, shall not be permitted" (Art. 11).[15]

CONCLUSION

It is clear that human rights documents, including the United Nations' Universal Declaration of Human Rights, condemn, sometimes explicitly, the cloning of human beings. They do so for good reasons. Human cloning would compromise the well-being and the moral status of the resulting child and would threaten human dignity generally. If we are to be true to human rights, and to the Universal Declaration proclaiming them, we should put this truth before the curiosity of science.

ENDNOTES

[1] The original article announcing the successful cloning of Dolly was published by Ian Wilmut, *et al.*, in *Nature* magazine 385 (1997): 810-813. Other popular scientific descriptions and discussions include: A. Coghlan, "One Small Step for a Sheep ..." *The New Scientist* 153, No. 2071 (1997): 4-5; P. Cohen, "We ask, they answer," *The New Scientist* 158, No. 2133 (1998): 26-35; and N. Boyce, "Go Forth and Multiply," *The New Scientist* 159, No. 2144 (1998): 4, 5.

[2] A clone is not 100 percent genetically identical to the nuclear donor. Certain structures in cells, the mitochondria, also contain some genetic material. A clone has the mitochondria of the egg cell that is used in the cloning process. The contribution of normal mitochondria DNA to "normal" traits is minimal, though defects in that DNA can lead to serious disorders.

[3] A Dutch paper recently reported that an American firm in the Bahamas, Valiant Venture, is offering a commercial service to clone both animals and humans on demand. The firm offers to store tissues precisely to make a clone

of a deceased child. *See* "Vrees voor genetische vuilnisbelt kleurt debat over klonen," *Het Financieele Dagblad,* July 17, 1998, p. 5.

[4] *See* publications of the National Bioethics Advisory Committee of the USA and the Group of Advisers on the Ethical Implications of Biotechnology to the European Commission. (For the executive summary of the former's findings and discussion of same, *see Hastings Center Report* 27, No. 5 (1997): 6-19; for a report on the latter, *see* "Ethical aspects of cloning techniques," Opinion of the Group of Advisers on the Ethical Implications of Biotechnology to the European Commission, No. 9, Brussels, Belgium, May 28, 1997.

[5] The terminology is problematic, of course. As a matter of biological fact, the creation of human embryos is the first step in human reproduction. This paper uses these terms only to describe the present debate and not to suggest the acceptability of any type of cloning, "non-reproductive" or otherwise.

[6] J.A. Tomson, *et al.,* "Embyronic Stem Cell Lines Derived from Human Blastocysts," *Science,* Vol. 282, 5391 (1998), p. 1145 ff; John D. Gearhart, *et al.,* "Derivation of Pluripotent Stem Cells from Cultured Human Primordial Germ Cells," Proceedings of the National Academy of Sciences, Vol. 95: 23, Washington, D.C., November 10, 1998. (Gearhart is actually the last author listed.) Gearhart used tissue from aborted fetuses. If it were possible to obtain embryonic stem cells from tissue of fetuses that aborted spontaneously, this would be an ethical alternative to culturing cells from embryos (presuming that embryos are viable if allowed to develop).

[7] M. Wadman, "Cloning without human clones," *The Wall Street Journal,* Jan 20, 1998. *See also* J. Stephenson, "Threatened Bans on Human Cloning Research could Hamper Advances," *JAMA* 277 (April 2, 1997): 1023-1026. Some scientists argued that even reproductive cloning should not be legally forbidden. *See* "Five Year Ban on Human Cloning in USA," *General Ethics News,* Issue 18, June/July 1997, p. 3. The National Bioethics Advisory Committee of the USA called for a five-year ban on reproductive cloning, but considered non-reproductive cloning ethically comparable to creating embryos for research and did not make a statement on that.

[8] *Supra* note 1.

[9] J. Duyndam, "Zorg en generositeit," in H. Manschot, M. Verkerk (red.), *Ethiek van de zorg,* Amsterdam: Boom 1994: 119-150. Duyndam refers to several works, including the research published by S.P. Onliner and P.M. Onliner in *The Altruistic Personality: Rescuers of Jews in Nazi Europe* (New York: Free Press, 1988).

[10] Preamble, The Universal Declaration of Human Rights.

[11] Preamble, The United Nations Convention on the Rights of the Child.

[12] *Bulletin of Medical Ethics,* May 1997: 10. The Council of Europe's *Convention for the Protection of Human Rights and Dignity of the Human Being with Regard to the Application of Biology and Medicine* also condemns the fully instrumental use of human embryos. Article 18 reads: (1) *Where the*

law allows research on embryos in vitro, *it shall ensure adequate protection of the embryo*; (2) *The creation of human embryos for research purposes is prohibited.*

[13] A.J. Heschel, *Wie is de mens? (Who Is Man?)* (Stanford, Calif.: Stanford University Press, 1965).

[14] Some of the points raised here are elaborated further by several authors, especially by G. Meilander and C.B. Mitchell in *Ethics & Medicine* 14, No. 1 (1998): 8-30.

[15] Other European institutions have also issued declarations on cloning. The Council of Europe published a protocol to the Convention for the Protection of Human Rights and Dignity of the Human Being with regard to the application of biology and medicine to the prohibition of cloning human beings. (The 1997 Convention, accepted by many European countries, did not contain any statement on cloning. Therefore, it was considered desirable to add a protocol on this topic.) This protocol was signed by 19 member states of the Council of Europe in January 1998. Article 1 states: "Any intervention seeking to create a human being genetically identical to another human being, whether living or dead, is prohibited." (*See Bulletin of Medical Ethics,* January 1998, at 4). Some countries, including The Netherlands, signed the protocol with the restriction that they interpreted it as a prohibition of reproductive cloning, not of the use of cloning in the context of research on embryos and ES cells (see text at 2). The Group of Advisers on the Ethical Implications of Biotechnology to the European Commission (see *supra* note 4) also rejected reproductive cloning but did not take an explicit position on non-reproductive cloning.

Chapter 6

The Role of the United Nations in International Drug Control

Irving Tragen

In June 1998, the United Nations (U.N.) General Assembly will hold its Second Special Session on the world's drug problem. Discussions will focus on the measures needed to bring the drug menace under control at national, regional and universal levels.

Like the League of Nations before it, the United Nations has been assigned a major role in combating the illegal production, traffic and use of narcotic drugs and psychotropic substances by its member states. The United Nations has evolved into the paramount international forum on the issue—the forum in which the bases for intergovernmental cooperation have been negotiated and formalized.

On the eve of this Special Session, it behooves us to look at what the United Nations has contributed to the anti-drug effort and to assess its relevance today for helping governments design and implement effective strategies and actions.

Irving G. Tragen is an international consultant on anti-drug programs. He served as the executive secretary for the Inter-American Drug Abuse Control Commission and worked in the Department of State and Organization of American States.

THE SIX-LINK CHAIN OF ORGANIZED DRUG CRIME

The drug problem is multi-dimensional. It is a complex chain of illicit trafficking, usually originating outside national borders and ending up with human beings enslaved in an addiction that denies them control over their lives or hope for the future.

This chain consists of six steps: (1) illicit production of crops or chemicals from which drugs are derived; (2) manufacturing or processing in laboratories which transform the raw material into illicit drugs; (3) clandestine transport of drugs to distribution centers and thence to the marketplace; (4) underground marketing of drugs to the user; (5) illicit consumption; and (6) laundering the profits generated by illicit sales. Most of the drugs are cultivated, produced, processed and manufactured outside the countries in which they are consumed. Today, there are few nations free of the specter of the addict, whether they be traditional producer, transit or consumer countries. Most crops from which drugs are derived can now be grown almost anywhere on the planet or substituted by synthetic substances made in rudimentary laboratories.

Over the past two decades, control of the drug chain has been taken over by powerful criminal organizations, such as the Italian and U.S. Mafias, the Colombian and Mexican Cartels, the Chinese Triads, the Japanese Yakusa, and the Russian Syndicates. These organizations, well-financed and fine-tuned by ruthless leaderships, have increasingly linked each of the six steps into elaborate, integrated businesses. Each organization retains its individual entity but forges closer ties with the others to facilitate cooperation in producing, processing, manufacturing and transporting drugs, and then in dividing up markets, and in laundering the money.

The drug trade generates enormous income for these criminal organizations. It allows them to take over legitimate businesses (including financial institutions), to corrupt governments, and to buy public support for their activities through social projects and public relations campaigns. Also, studies show that profit margins escalate sharply as the product gets closer to the marketplace.[1] Thus, the user in the large, consuming countries is the primary contributor to the profits of this organized crime.

Measures to bring this problem under control have been debated for most of this century. For too long, the debate was whether the traffic was supply- or demand-driven: Countries plagued by drug use accused the producer and transit countries of not curtailing the supply; producer and transit countries blamed user countries for not reducing the demand. This debate hindered inter-country cooperation for decades, to the exclusive benefit of the drug traffickers who raked in their profits.

It was only in the mid-1980s that consensus was reached between consumer and producer countries that supply and demand are two halves of the same problem. To bring it under control, each and every link in the chain (from production to money laundering) needed to be systematically suppressed. New strategies then emerged that drew consumer, transit and producer countries together, for a coordinated effort, with priority given to measures that disrupt the profit flow to the criminal organizations, which would undermine their capability to control the drug supply and marketing network. This strategy called for significant reduction of production and consumption. The United Nations proved to be one of the most important fora for building world-wide acceptance of this new strategy.

THE HISTORICAL AND PRESENT FRAMEWORK OF THE U.N. PROGRAM

For more than a century, the problem of drug addiction has led governments to seek bases for international cooperation to impede the flows into their territories. The seeds of international concern were sown by Britain's victory in the mid-nineteenth century Opium War, which accorded it a monopoly over opium imports into China, where consumption had been previously forbidden. From China, opium use spread to the major seaports of Western Europe, especially London, which, ironically, awakened international efforts to outlaw opium use.

International cooperation to combat opium traffic dates from the 1909 Shanghai Conference, which culminated in the 1912 Hague Convention. The Hague Convention was essentially a voluntary undertaking by signatory governments to prevent illegal trading in opium. Article 23 of the League of Nations' Charter gave it the responsibility for "general supervision over the execution of agreements with regard to ... the traffic in opium and other dangerous drugs." Three additional conventions were adopted by the League of Nations in response to the growing concern of the world community to this problem. These conventions, and the League's increased responsibilities in the area, broadened the League's authority to coordinate intergovernmental actions to suppress not only opium and its derivative, heroin, but also two other families of narcotic drugs:

cocaine, which is derived from coca leaves, and cannabis, popularly called marijuana.

When the United Nations was created after World War II, it assumed the mandates of the League on illicit drug trafficking. In 1946, the Economic and Social Council of the United Nations (ECOSOC) created the Commission on Narcotic Drugs (CND) and its secretariat, the Division of Narcotic Drugs (DND), to carry out these functions.

THE UNITED NATIONS CONVENTIONS

By the mid-1950s, the CND noted serious contradictions and ambiguities among the existing conventions and, in 1959, was empowered to revise and consolidate them. This consolidation process produced the Single Convention of 1961, as amended by the Protocol of 1972. It set up a world-wide system to control the cultivation, production, manufacture, export, import, distribution, trade, use and possession of all three families of narcotic drugs: opium, coca leaf, cannabis, and their derivatives.

By the mid-1960s, illicit international traffickers had expanded their wares from these three narcotic drugs to include new substances, the psychotropics. Produced naturally or synthetically in laboratories, psychotropics induce dependency and produce central nervous system stimulation or depression, and result in hallucinations or disturbances in motor function, thinking, behavior, perception or mood. To address these new substances, the 1971 Convention on Psychotropic Substances was adopted. It established world-wide machinery to limit and control their production and marketing.

Both U.N. Conventions established annual limits on the production of the designated drugs to the amounts needed for medical and scientific purposes, as well as controls on their shipment and marketing. Unfortunately, clandestine production, marketing and distribution paralleled the mechanism set up under the Conventions. These clandestine operations assumed world-wide dimensions and, dominated by powerful criminal cartels, frustrated efforts to enforce the two Conventions.

In 1984, Colombia and Venezuela, deeply concerned about the power of illicit traffickers and the disruption and corruption they spawned, proposed that a new Convention be prepared to deal with illicit traffic in narcotic drugs and psychotropic substances. The result was the 1988 United Nations Convention Against Illicit Traffic in Narcotic Drugs and Psychotropic Substances, also known as the 1988 Convention of Vienna.

These three Conventions form the framework of the U.N. anti-drug effort. All three have been ratified and implemented by most of the governments of the world.

THE 1988 CONVENTION OF VIENNA

The 1988 Convention of Vienna establishes legal principles and procedures for intergovernmental cooperation for suppressing illicit drug trafficking. Its 34 articles were negotiated in less than four years, which is record time for so controversial an international accord that reconciled not only conflicting national perceptions about the nature of the problem, but also the different norms and procedures of Civil, Common, Muslim, Eastern Bloc, Asian and other legal systems. As of February 1998, the 1988 Convention of Vienna has been ratified by 143 countries, encompassing 75 percent of the countries of the world, including all western hemisphere countries, 82 percent of Europe, 70 percent of Africa, 71 percent of Asia and 21 percent of Oceania.

The Convention was designed "to promote cooperation among the parties so that they may address more effectively the various aspects of illicit traffic in narcotic drugs and psychotropic substances having an international dimension."[2] The parties to the Convention committed themselves to work together and to enact necessary domestic legislation to effect the Convention's goals.

The Convention obligates its parties to establish the following as criminal offenses in their respective jurisdictions: (1) all activities that contravene the provisions of the other two U.N. Conventions; and (2) all intentional acts in the chain of drug trafficking, including cultivation, production, manufacture, extraction, preparation, offering, offering for sale, distribution, sale, delivery on any terms, brokerage, dispatch in transit, transport, and exportation or importation of narcotic drugs and psychotropic substances, as well as their use and possession. It covers the manufacture, transport and distribution of equipment, materials and specific substances used in the illicit cultivation, production or manufacture of illegal drugs. Also defined as offenses are the management or financing of illicit activities, including the conversion or transfer of property, money laundering, and participating or conspiring knowingly therein. Each country, in accordance with its constitution and legal system, commits itself to combating and suppressing each of these offenses and to applying sanctions against wrongdoers.

The Convention also sets the first international guidelines for shaping domestic legislation on asset seizure from drug traffickers and their allies, money laundering, and forfeiture of proceeds derived from drug trafficking.[3] In addition, it spells out rules and procedures for dealing with the diversion of precursor chemicals and other essential chemical substances from licit to illicit uses.[4] It further recommends measures to eradicate illicit cultivation and to reduce demand.[5] It specifically authorizes parties to adopt more severe or strict measures than those set forth in the Convention.[6]

The Convention provides the bases for intergovernmental cooperation by: (1) spelling out the jurisdiction of the parties over criminal actions in complex international situations;[7] (2) setting ground rules for extradition; (3) defining areas of mutual legal assistance and other forms of judicial, police and technical cooperation;[8] (4) establishing rules and procedures for handling drug cases in special situations (such as in free trade zones and free ports, on the high seas, and in postal systems);[9] and (5) prescribing rules for handling drug shipments by merchant ships and commercial carriers and the proper labeling of such exports.[10]

The three Conventions, however, do not delegate enforcement powers to U.N. agencies. It is left to member countries to enact necessary domestic laws and enforce them. The U.N. is limited to administrative measures and informing the world community about noncompliance.[11] Therefore, successful implementation of the Conventions depends on the capability and will of national governments.

ADMINISTRATION OF THE CONVENTIONS

The Economic and Social Council (ECOSOC) of the United Nations is the political body that sets policy for world-wide anti-drug programs. In turn, ECOSOC has delegated the authority to implement, or recommend changes for, such programs to the Commission of Narcotic Drugs (CND). CND meets annually in Vienna and is made up of 54 member states elected to three-year terms. Its executive committee usually meets two or more times each year.

The CND has sponsored regional bodies to facilitate consultation and cooperation in various parts of the world. The first of these was the

Sub-Commission in Illicit Drug Traffic and Related Matters in the Near and Middle East, established in 1973. In the other regions starting in 1974, Heads of National Law Enforcement Agencies (HONLEAs) were progressively set up for Asia and the Pacific, Latin America and the Caribbean, Africa and Europe. The Sub-Commission and HONLEAs have traditionally met annually, and they join together every third year in a world-wide session. For officials of many developing countries, HONLEAs serve as their principal source of information on drug-traffic trends and conditions. In the Western Hemisphere, the 34 active member states of the Organization of America States (OAS) set up their own forum and program, namely the Inter-American Drug Abuse Control Commission (CICAD).

The Secretariat that services the CND and administers the U.N. drug program is the United Nations International Drug Control Program (UNDCP). Headquartered in Vienna, it was created in 1990 by merging three existing agencies: (1) the Division of Narcotic Drugs (DND), created in 1946 to serve as the Secretariat for the Commission; (2) the International Narcotics Control Board (INCB), established in 1961 under the Single Convention as an expert body to assess the world drug situation and to propose necessary measures to improve the effectiveness of anti-drug efforts; and (3) the Fund for Drug Abuse Control (UNFDAC), created in 1971 to receive voluntary contributions by member states and invest them in approved anti-drug programs. UNDCP absorbed the functions of the DND and UNFDAC while the INCB retained its autonomy with technical and clerical support provided by UNDCP.

UNDCP is one of the smaller U.N. agencies. It is staffed by no more than a couple of hundred professional, legal, technical, administrative and clerical personnel. This staff is frequently reinforced by short-term national experts lent by governments. Essentially it is a core staff of specialists and program managers that services the CND and works with member governments in applying the conventions. It relies on other U.N. Specialized Agencies for expertise on important aspects of the drug problem, including the Food and Agriculture Organization (FAO) on crop substitution; the World Health Organization (WHO) on drug abuse and other health issues; and the United Nations Education, Science and Culture Organization (UNESCO) on drug prevention and educational questions. Unfortunately, each of these Specialized Agencies has its own priorities, among which drug control is not the highest, and their anti-drug efforts depend essentially on project funds that UNDCP provides them.

One of UNDCP's most effective components is the International Narcotics Control Board (INCB), composed of 13 experts elected for five year terms. Board members are chosen for their expertise. They are not representatives for their nations. INCB systematically assesses the drug situation throughout the world and reports annually to the CND on the progress made, on the current obstacles to combating drugs, as well as on the implementation of key provisions of the three Conventions. INCB also coordinates world-wide efforts to suppress illicit traffic in precursor and other chemicals essential for the manufacture of narcotic drugs. For more than 30 years, INCB annual reports have provided a comprehensive and objective record of anti-drug efforts at worldwide, regional and national levels.

TECHNICAL ASSISTANCE

From 1946 to 1971, the U.N. anti-drug program revolved around CND meetings, as well as reports of the INCB (after its creation in 1961). The United Nations also provided periodic training courses for national officials on the provisions of the conventions, collection and analysis of necessary statistics, preparation of national reports, operations of forensic laboratories, and other selected subjects mandated by the CND.

After 1971, with the growing concern of the world community about illicit drug trafficking and increasing use of narcotic drugs and psychotropic substances by youth, the member states established UNFDAC as an autonomous body to administer a voluntary fund for financing technical assistance projects. These were designed to help less developed countries implement priority anti-drug programs. The Fund supported its own staff of specialists and program managers as well those technicians needed for in-country technical advice and help. Voluntary contributions to UNFDAC were initially minuscule. However, funding increased substantially in the 1980s, recently reaching $60-70 million a year. This gave UNFDAC a significant role in the U.N. anti-drug programs. The scope of these programs and their priority areas have been set by the principal founders: namely, Canada, Germany, Italy, Scandinavia, the United Kingdom, the United States, and other Western European countries. Only limited contributions have come from developing countries.

UNFDAC priorities were focused on those aspects of the drug problem found in developing countries. The first was to reduce production of the three families of narcotic drugs proscribed under the Single Convention of 1961, through crop substitution and other grass-roots programs to induce farmers to curtail production. The second was to improve law enforcement in producer and transit countries to disrupt the illicit transit of drugs. The third was to increase the capability of governments to administer anti-drug programs. Projects in crop substitution involving thousands of peasant farmers in the Middle East, Southeast Asia, and Latin America were very expensive and absorbed most of UNFDAC's resources.

Despite considerable localized success, the results did not appreciably reduce supply, and areas that ceased producing were replaced by others in the same or neighboring countries to satisfy the growing demand in the major consuming centers such as the United States and Western Europe. An axiom of elementary economics is that demand begets supply and that, when demand is strong and profit margins high, someone will satisfy that demand until the risks outweigh the lure of profits. UNFDAC's experience illustrated the applicability of this axiom to the drug problem. There was a need to take commensurate and coordinated measures to reduce both demand and supply.

UNFDAC's priorities reflected the strategies used in most Western countries, which were then based on the premise that demand for drugs was supply-driven and that the problem could be solved by cutting off the supply. Little comprehensive attention was given to demand reduction until the mid-1980s when Nancy Reagan called on the United States to commit itself to a national effort to save our youth from drugs and to make drug use morally and socially unacceptable behavior.

Since its creation in 1990, UNDCP has assumed the functions of UNFDAC and has redefined priorities. Priorities currently include advice and assistance to governments on measures needed to: (1) implement and comply with the 1988 Convention of Vienna; (2) enhance cooperation among countries in combating drug trafficking. This new focus has substantially reduced the investment of funds in crop substitution, but not in law enforcement and other governmental anti-drug agencies. To date, UNDCP has made few investments in demand reduction projects, which still are not the primary concern of developing countries even though the use of narcotic drugs and psychotropic substances in many producer and transit countries has risen sharply and is now ranked among the most serious social and law enforcement problems.

UNDCP has had the Comprehensive Multidisciplinary Outline of Future Activities in Drug Abuse Control (the CMO, adopted in Vienna in June 1987 at a conference convened by the CND and attended by representatives of 138 states) at its disposal to develop its programs and priorities. The CMO details courses of action needed at national, regional and world-wide levels to reduce supply and demand, combat drug trafficking, and promote inter-country cooperation.

The UNDCP can also call upon a score of intergovernmental bodies, and more than 200 non-governmental organizations for advice and guidance.

The priorities and programs of UNDCP are set by the member states not only in the CND but through actions taken in other arenas. For example, when, in Paris in 1989, the G-7 Chiefs of State recognized the problem of money laundering and the threat posed by enormous profits from drug trafficking (which organized crime laundered clandestinely), it established a special task force, the Financial Action Task Force (FATF), to address the problem. Now FATF, not UNDCP, has responsibility to follow up on recommendations approved by the G-7. FATF operates out of the Organization for Economic Development (OECD) in Paris, not in Vienna with UNDCP. UNDCP is only one of several international groups that serve as FATF Advisors, despite the provisions of the 1988 Convention of Vienna.

On the other hand, in 1990 the G-7 established another task force, the Chemical Action Task Force (CATF), to make recommendations on how to disrupt the traffic in precursor and other chemicals essential for the processing and manufacture of narcotic drugs and psychotropic substances. When the CATF completed its work, the G-7 turned to UNDCP to integrate its recommendations into the related work already underway by the INCB.

THE ROLE OF THE UNITED NATIONS

Analyzing the history and record of the United Nations in combating narcotic drugs clearly establishes that its role has been: (1) to be the forum for world discussion; (2) to be the mechanism for negotiating and formulating conventions; (3) to provide advice to governments on how to comply with the conventions; (4) to collect and disseminate information and statistics on the drug problem; and (5) to provide technical assistance and training for national officials.

In the CND, the central U.N. forum on drugs, greater attention each year is being given to the strategies and measures needed to reduce demand, including both prevention and treatment and rehabilitation of users. Article 3, paragraph 2, of the 1988 Convention of Vienna establishes "the possession, purchase or cultivation of narcotic drugs or psychotropic substances for personal consumption" as a criminal offense, but allows member states, in accordance with their respective legal systems, to establish the sanctions, which may range from severe penalties to drug treatment and education. This discretion reflects the various positions of countries in the negotiations. Some states (i.e., some Muslim countries) called for the death penalty for drug users; others called for imprisonment, others for treatment, and a small group of countries only wanted a light slap on the wrist.

The provisions of the 1988 Convention of Vienna have governed official discussions in the CND in recent years. Some corridor debates have become bitter. Advocates of decriminalization of drugs are well-financed and supported by European cities such as Amsterdam, Frankfurt, Hamburg and Zurich. They assert that such action would break the hold of the criminal organizations over drug trafficking and, by taxing the sale of these drugs, would provide the revenues needed to cover the cost of expanded prevention and treatment program. The majority view, supported by almost all governments, many non-governmental organizations, and European Cities Against Drugs, is that legalization would set back prevention and treatment efforts and legitimize drug traffickers. The majority points to the experience of Sweden. There, intensive prevention and information programs for youth have been sustained along-side strict law enforcement and obligatory treatment for users. This has not only reduced drug use, but also has reduced crime rates and the public health costs of treating drug addicts.

For the United Nations and the world community, demand reduction has become the pivotal topic. Drug use and its accompanying crimes have filled the prisons of many countries. The prevention of future use is both a moral imperative and a significant contribution to crime reduction. The definition of prevention needs to encompass both the non-user and the treatment and rehabilitation of users. Giving a government's seal of respectability to drug use, through decriminalization or legalization, hardly seems a logical base for this.

THE ROLE OF MEMBER STATES

To reduce demand, the primary actors will be governments, not the United Nations. It is evident from the above that the United Nations' role is to support governments and promote cooperation among them. Governments reserve to themselves the powers needed to: (1) curtail cultivation, production, processing and manufacturing operations; (2) disrupt domestic and international traffic; (3) reduce drug use; (4) suppress money laundering; and (5) dismantle criminal organizations. The member states, acting alone or in concert with other governments under bilateral agreements, are the actors in this arena. If they seek international support for a specific operation, they are more likely to turn to INTERPOL or the Customs Cooperation Council, rather than UNDCP.

Member governments define the philosophy, strategy, policies and agenda for the United Nations, the UNDCP, the U.N. General Assembly, the ECOSOC and the DNC. Changes in philosophy, strategy, policies and agenda come only after negotiation among the member states and the coalescing of consensus. If any such changes are to be announced at the Second Special Session of the General Assembly, they most probably have already been substantially agreed to in prior negotiations.

The Second Special Session of the General Assembly will be the venue for disseminating those decisions already agreed upon by the meeting states. At the First Special Session of the General Assembly in February 1989, its final report (*Political Declaration and Global Programme of Action for the United Nations Decade against Drug Abuse 1991-2000*), spelled out priority actions that governments should take. It then assigned complementary and supporting responsibilities to regional and world-wide organizations. It, in fact, recognized that each and every member government bears the primary responsibility for suppressing illicit drug traffic and drug use.

The other dimension of the Second Special Session will be the opportunity for member states to reaffirm their commitments to combat drug traffic and drug abuse and publicize their national strategies and programs. The world community can hope for the commitment by every government to make a sustained effort, individually and in concert with all other members, to attack each and every link in the drug traffic chain as long as the problem persists. Such a commitment has special significance for the people of North America and Europe, whose users are the source of profits for organized crime and whose youth are most at risk. The commitment should be nothing less than making the use of narcotic drugs and psychotropic substances morally and socially unacceptable behavior. The United Nations, as well as member states, should sanction the failure to live up to these commitments by the loss of the right to participate in the United Nations. Only with such seriousness can the world successfully rid itself of the drug plague it now suffers.

ENDNOTES

[1] Irving G. Tragen et al., Socio-Economic Studies for the Inter-American Specialized Conference on Drug Trafficking (Organization of American States 1986) Section 1 at 21-22.

[2] The 1988 Convention of Vienna, Article 2, par. 1.

[3] *Id.*, Article 3, sec. 1(c), and Article 5.

[4] *Id.*, Article 12.

[5] *Id.*, Article 14.

[6] *Id.*, Article 24.

[7] *Id.*, Article 6.

[8] *Id.*, Articles 7-9.

[9] *Id.*, Articles 16-19.

[10] *Id.*, Article 15.

[11] *Id.*, Articles 20-23.

Chapter 7

Drug Legalization and the United Nations' Universal Declaration of Human Rights

Franziska Haller

On December 10, 1948, the General Assembly of the United Nations adopted the Universal Declaration of Human Rights. For the first time in history, and only after lengthy preparations, the international community agreed upon universal norms to safeguard security, freedom, and peace. While the application of these norms is not yet a reality around our world, each nation has the Declaration as its goal, and each state must try, by its constitution and by its laws, to guarantee its promises and recognize that "[e]veryone has the right to life, liberty and security of person"[1]; and that "[e]veryone is entitled to a social and international order in which the rights and freedoms set forth in this Declaration can be fully realized."[2]

Unfortunately, the plague of drug abuse, and the possibility of drug legalization, are grave threats to these basic human rights. This paper is a discussion of these threats and how the United Nations (U.N.), and its member nations, can counter them.

Franziska Haller, Ph.D., is a pharmacist and psychologist. She has served as an expert at the United Nations on the issue of drug craving and on the Swiss Federal Commission on Narcotic Drugs.

THE EVIL OF DRUG ADDICTION

No form of slavery is worse than drug addiction. While drugs can, and often do, inflict permanent damage to the body, they primarily affect the user's brain. Drugs alter feelings, thought processes, and behavior. The ability to make decisions wanes, as does self-discipline. The user eventually loses inner freedom and, with it, human dignity.

In addition to the user's suffering, there is the suffering of family and friends, who must witness the user's self-destruction and deterioration. They are left to watch the all-consuming nature of drug addiction. Too often, they must observe the descent into crime, violence, or other risky and harmful behaviors that mark the life of the addict. Such experiences are great psychological and physical ordeals, and they cause serious tensions within the home and within the larger community. (Indeed, both the United Nations and the Pontifical Council on the Family have stressed how drug abuse, and the concomitant weakening and eventual breakdown of the family, constitute an existential danger to our society.[3])

The growth of the drug problem and our so-called modern *zeitgeist* are closely intertwined. For 30 years, certain forces have worked to change, if not destroy, the traditional morals of society in Western Europe. As a result, people today are more preoccupied with independence and with autonomy. They are more isolated in their sovereign, autonomous worlds and less grounded in relationships. There is little talk of moral obligations to others, and even less effort to recognize or honor such obligations.

This has created great confusion and insecurity among people, especially among our young. Their insecurity, combined with loneliness, fear, the desire for acceptance, and other factors, provides fertile soil for the use and spread of drugs.

BYPRODUCTS OF THE DRUG CULTURE AND THE DRUG TRADE

Once addiction sets in, matters get worse. It is only with the help of drugs, and often for the sake of drugs alone, that people around the world are slaughtered and murdered in an endless cycle of drug production, distribution, sale, and consumption. Drugs dismantle natural inhibitions, rendering users more explosive and violent when under their influence. The desperation of addiction, too, leads to violent and criminal conduct simply to obtain more drugs.

Even children are given drugs to make them tools in the drug trade, among other things. The Preamble to the 1988 Vienna Convention gives some indication of the severity of this problem. It asserts that signing parties are "[d]eeply concerned ... particularly by the fact that children are used in many parts of the world as an illicit drug consumers market and for purposes of illicit production, distribution and trade in narcotic drugs and psychotropic substances. ... This ... entails a danger of incalculable gravity."[4] Needless to say, when a problem threatens even our very young this way, we have a tragedy at hand.

THE INTERNATIONAL EFFORT TO COMBAT DRUG ABUSE

From the very beginning, the United Nations has made the struggle against drugs a central concern. It realized early on that, "[w]hen a substantial percentage of any generation is addicted, that generation has lost contributing citizens and has acquired a crippling social burden."[5] The involvement of the United Nations is all the more fitting as time goes on, since the drug problem is now unquestionably a global matter.

This borderless character of the drug scourge has always encouraged countries to stem the drug tide with international agreements. For decades, countries focused on adopting effective treaties. Thus, three complementary conventions now exist: (1) The 1961 Single Convention on Narcotic Drugs (as amended by the 1972 Protocol); (2) The 1971 Convention on Psychotropic Substances; and (3) The 1988 Convention against Illicit Traffic on Narcotic Drugs and Psychotropic Substances. [6] Most countries have ratified these conventions. In addition, the U.N. General Assembly plans to adopt a Declaration on Demand Reduction this year, in special session.

The 1961 Single Convention unequivocally favored firm action against drugs. It stated: "[A]ddiction to narcotic drugs constitutes a serious evil for the individual and is fraught with social and economic danger to mankind." It further asserted that signing parties should be "conscious of their duty to prevent and combat this evil."[7] There simply can be no question that the United Nations, as well as the larger international community, has historically and laudably been a strong voice speaking out against drugs and drug abuse.

Despite this international consensus, however, some nations have begun to send the wrong message, sending our youth in the wrong direction. The drug policies in Switzerland and the Netherlands, for example, are *de facto* legalization of marijuana, which clearly violates the spirit of these international conventions, as does Switzerland's direct heroin distribution program, discussed at length below.

Such policies and practices fly in the face of an almost axiomatic truth: Increased availability of drugs means increased likelihood of drug consumption. Legalization, liberalization, decriminalization, or the more euphemistic description, "medically controlled distribution," of drugs, all amount to the same thing: increased availability. This inevitably results in increased consumption, especially tragic among our young, who could well perceive such policies as effective invitations to narcotic use.

THE SWISS MODEL AND THE UNITED NATIONS

Despite the evidence that strict curbs on drugs are most effective in fighting the abuse problem, proponents of legalization continue to claim that we must find "new ways" to combat drug addiction. Legalization and regulation, they claim, comprise the solution.

Unfortunately, Switzerland has played into the hands of these proponents. It now stands as the only country in the world to distribute heroin on such a large scale. This practice forms part of an official policy called "harm reduction," whose eventual goal is the blanket legalization of all drugs. Proponents intend to use the so called "Swiss model" (which is nothing less than state distribution of heroin) as a model solution for the world in the war against drugs.

In 1992, the Swiss Federal Government agreed to seven projects that began in December 1993 and involved the government itself overseeing heroin distribution to addicts. The number of projects quickly multiplied, however, as did the number of heroin recipients. The areas of research then changed and expanded, so that proponents even managed to launch one such "project" in a prison, and yet another with psychiatric drug-addicted patients. Experiment subjects changed constantly, as did the allocation of drugs to them, and there were no control groups at all.

To state the obvious, such changes are enormously significant for an experiment that is supposed to be scientific and from which major policy changes could emerge. The Swiss projects have become mere vehicles through which legalization proponents can foist their preferred practices on a nation, with no verifiable benefit to addicts or to society.

The trial is like a railway station where travelers arrive and depart as they please, with no direction or help given to them.

The effect of these pilot projects on conventional, abstinence-oriented therapy has been overwhelmingly negative. Heroin distribution is an easy, undemanding alternative to traditional treatment. It is no surprise that addicts prefer it. As a result, beds in traditional therapy centers are empty, and the risk of closing down such institutions completely is very real.[8] Morale has declined because the mission has been made more difficult: Amidst the public policy message that drug use is okay (even promoted by the state), simply motivating addicts to abstain from drug use is now an arduous task. In addition, the major media relentlessly favor liberalization and legalization. Given all this, the prospects for sound therapy and prevention efforts look bleak indeed.

To their credit, the United Nations, and its various drug combating agencies, have remained critical of the Swiss model and have even warned other countries against following suit:

It is the Board's opinion that no Government should accept the proliferation of such trials. Otherwise the world would, under the cover of science and medicine, move along a path leading to legalization of the non-medical use of drugs. ... [I]n reality, the search for quick fixes is the result of political neglect in the past. ... [For too long] there was a very tolerant attitude and a delay in activating the necessary financial and human resources for efforts in demand reduction, particularly in primary prevention and in law enforcement. ... [T]he unusual and extensive media coverage afforded to such trials, including the unequivocal statement of some politicians who described the trials as being a first step towards legalization, may have already had a negative impact on preventive programs, by way of contributing to an increasing social acceptance of heroin.[9]

The Vienna Convention of 1988 also clearly states that such public propaganda of narcotic drugs is to be a punishable offense, a policy that is reinforced and supported by the International Narcotics Control Board. In 1997, this Board's report reiterated: "Article 3 of the United Nations Convention against Illicit Traffic in Narcotic Drugs and Psychotropic Substances of 1988 refers to *publicly inciting or inducing others, by any means, to commit any of the offenses established in accordance with this article or to use narcotic drugs or psychotropic substances illicitly* (subparagraph 1 (c) (iii)) *and requires each party to* establish such conduct as a criminal offense under its domestic law."[10]

Given such strong sentiments, supporters of the Swiss model would do well to rethink their approach to the evil of drug addiction.

THE PRESENT AND THE FUTURE

Opposition to official drug distribution (the Swiss model) and to drug legalization remains strong to this day. This was clear during the 1997 Commission on Narcotic Drugs: Not a single country supported the legalization/distribution approach to the drug problem. In 1998, again, the condemnation was firm:

> [I]t has always been the fear of the Board that such a project will be a bad example for other countries. This has already been the case in some other European countries. Such a proliferation of heroin distribution to heroin addicts is not in line with the policy of this Commission and therefore not acceptable. This concern was also expressed here by a number of other countries like Poland, Sweden, United States and others and I am confident that many delegations share that concern. The Board stated its position in its 1996 and 1997 reports and has nothing to add for the time being.[11]

The Pontifical Council for the Family has also stressed the problems with the "Swiss model," highlighting the evil nature of drug addiction and the folly of policies which appear to accept it:

> No one will deny that the use of drugs is an evil. It does not matter if they are purchased illegally or distributed by the state: in both cases they are destructive for the human being. ... Some people's lives are affected or injured while other [people]—perhaps without becoming really addicted—destroy their youth and are no longer capable of developing their real abilities. ... The behavior which leads to drug addiction cannot improve if the substances that encourage this very behavior are freely available.[12]

All these statements are, of course, to the good. At the same time, however, it is vital that the United Nations expose and denounce violations of its conventions more publicly and more vehemently. The United Nations must insist on compliance with the conventions in its diplomatic dealings. If the drug problem really is to be solved—and this is possible—the international community cannot let a single country go the way of drug legalization, no matter how strident the claims of "medical benefit" and "science" become.

Of course, the United Nations alone cannot make drugs go away. The drug control conventions will be only as effective as member states make them. Each nation and government must undertake "any possible effort to reduce the availability of illegal drugs."[13] Only with an all-out effort of this kind can we realize the promise of the Universal Declaration of Human Rights and secure "a social and international order in which [the Declaration's freedoms] can be fully realized."[14]

ENDNOTES

[1] The United Nations' Universal Declaration of Human Rights, Article 3.

[2] *Id.,* Article 28.

[3] The United Nations and Drug Abuse Control, United Nations, New York (1989), p. 39; Pontifical Council of the Family, *Von der Hoffnung zur Hoffnungslosigkeit, Familie und Drogenabhangigkeit,* Libreria Editrice Vaticana (1992), pp. 25, 28.

[4] United Nations Convention Against Illicit Traffic in Narcotic Drugs and Psychotropic Substances (1988), Preamble.

[5] The United Nations and Drug Abuse Control, United Nations, New York (1989), p. 15.

[6] "[R]ecognizing the need to reinforce and supplement the measures provided in the Single Convention on Narcotic Drugs, 1961, that Convention is amended by the 1972 Protocol Amending the Single Convention on Narcotic Drugs, 1961, and the 1971 Convention on Psychotropic Substances." United Nations' Convention against Illicit Traffic on Narcotic Drugs and Psychotropic Substances (1988), Preamble.

[7] Single Convention on Narcotic Drugs (1961), Preamble.

[8] Martin Kull, Speech, *Nationalen Treffen Jugend ohne Drogen,* Bern, Switzerland, March 28, 1998.

[9] Dr. O. Schroeder, President, International Narcotics Control Board, Statement at 39th Session of the Commission on Narcotic Drugs (16-25 April 1996). The International Narcotics Control Board (INCB) and the Commission on Narcotic Drugs (CND) have sharply criticized state legalization of heroin. At the 1996 U.N. Commission on Narcotic Drugs in Vienna, many discussed and criticized the Swiss heroin projects. The INCB (and several countries) also questioned their scientific and medical validity. [The Commission on Narcotic Drugs was founded in 1946 as a functional commission of the Economic and Social Council (ECOSOC). "It is the central policy-making body within the United Nations system for dealing in depth with all questions

related to drug abuse control." The United Nations and Drug Abuse Control, United Nations, New York (1989), p. 79. The International Narcotics Control Board (INCB) was created by the Single Convention of 1961 and is aimed at effectively limiting the cultivation of plants containing psychotropic substances, as well as eliminating the production and illicit use of drugs. (The use of drugs for medical and scientific purposes is guaranteed.)]

[10] Report, International Narcotics Control Board (1997), p. 2.

[11] Statement, Dr. O. Schroeder, Member, International Narcotics Board, 41st Session of the Commission on Narcotic Drugs, March 13, 1998. It is noteworthy, too, that the INCB no longer describes the Swiss model as a "trial." It unequivocally calls it what it is: "heroin distribution."

[12] Pontifical Council of the Family, *von der Hoffnung zur Hoffnungslosigkeit, Familie und Drogenabhangigkeit, Libreria Editrice Vaticana* 1992, p. 21.

[13] Single Convention of 1961 as amended by the Protocol of 1972 and the 1988 Convention.

[14] *Supra* note 2.

Chapter 8

China's *Laogai*: A Gross Human Rights Violation

Harry Wu

The General Assembly of the United Nations adopted the Universal Declaration of Human Rights in 1948. In 1949, the Communist Party, headed by Mao Tse Tung, took control of China and remains in control to this day. The violations of the Universal Declaration are as great now as they were then.

This essay discusses human rights violations in China. Despite claims that China is now somehow different from what it was in the past, it remains a country that prohibits free expression and punishes political dissent. In sum, it is a country whose people do not enjoy the most basic of human rights that the Universal Declaration sought to guarantee.

Harry Wu is executive director of the Laogai Research Foundation and a research fellow at the Hoover Institution at Stanford University. As a former political prisoner who spent 19 years in the labor camps in China, Mr. Wu now seeks to expose human rights abuses there.

DENG'S CHINA LIVES ON

Deng Xiaoping died this past spring, but the Chinese communism and totalitarianism he oversaw lives on. Many suggest that conditions improved under his watch, for he opened the door to foreign investment, and some Chinese have even become rich. But those who claim that human rights are now observed in China are unaware of the truth of Chinese life. While it is true that Deng allowed some capitalism to flourish, and Mao would never have tolerated that, it is also true that Deng maintained Mao's politics of despotism. Anyone who contends otherwise should take a close look at my country, where the state attempts to control not just vast resources and the means of production, but the human spirit as well.

Article 5 of the United Nations' Universal Declaration of Human Rights states, "No one shall be subject to torture or cruel, inhuman or degrading treatment or punishment." I can personally attest to the egregious and continual breach of this promise, as can countless others.

We need only look at the cases of a group I call "The Three *W*s." I am the first *W*. In 1957, while I was attending university in Beijing, I spoke against the Soviet Union's invasion of Hungary. For this, I was labeled a "counterrevolutionary" and sent in 1960 to the forced labor camps, known to the Chinese people as the *Laogai*. I spent 19 years in such camps.

While there, I endured beatings, torture, and near starvation. Other prisoners found suicide preferable to continued existence under these conditions. Since my release in 1979, I have studied the *Laogai* closely and have tried to monitor and expose them through the work of the *Laogai* foundations in Washington, D.C., and in California. In the past 25 years, I have seen no evidence of changes in *Laogai* conditions. On the contrary, the present Chinese Communist Party is as intolerant of political dissent, and as severe in punishing it with forced labor, as any predecessor regime.

In 1979 (the year I emerged from the *Laogai*), the second *W*, Wei Jingsheng, a Chinese democracy rights activist, was sentenced to 15 years in the *Laogai* for suggesting in public that China needed democracy. In 1989, the third *W*, Wang Dan, a student advocate of democracy, received a four-year sentence for being a leader of the 1989 Tiananmen Square protests. I was in the United States at that time, and Wei Jingsheng was in the tenth year of his sentence.

Thus, the Chinese government initially sentenced each *W* in one of three different decades. We all received second sentences for equally innocuous "crimes" in the 1990s, the supposed era of improved human rights observance.

After releasing Wei Jingsheng in 1993, Chinese authorities arrested him again in 1994 and sentenced him to 14 more years in prison. Wang Dan, upon his release, hoped to enroll at the University of California at Berkeley. Instead, he was forced to return to prison: A Chinese court had found him guilty of "subverting the government" because he wrote an article critical of the regime. His sentence was 11 years.

I, too, was sentenced a second time for "stealing state secrets." Fortunately, I was an American citizen by this time. It was only because of this that the despots in Beijing expelled me from China rather than insist that I serve the 15-year sentence they gave me in August 1995. Happily, the two remaining *W*s were also exiled to the United States: Wei Jingsheng in November of 1997 and Wang Dan in April of 1998. But this should not cloud the reality of what the current Chinese regime is: a totalitarian communist system. Installed under Mao, this system has changed little over the years in its oppressive nature, despite economic developments.

FEAR OF HUMAN RIGHTS: THE *LAOGAI* AS A TOOL OF OPPRESSION

China's leaders have a deep-seeded fear of real democracy and human rights. It is common knowledge that tyrannical systems need methods of suppression to maintain power. Hitler had his concentration camps, and Stalin had his gulags. Similarly, since the dawn of the People's Republic, Chinese authorities have had their *Laogai*. The word *Laogai* literally means "reform through labor," but it has come to stand for Beijing's vast system of politically imposed slavery. It has proved itself an effective tool in maintaining political control.

The fundamental mentality of the *Laogai* today is "forced labor the means, while thought reform is the goal." The camps serve to punish and reform criminals in a manner that is useful for the state. More specifically, the Chinese Communist Party's economic theory postulates that human beings are essentially and primarily "productive forces" and should be used accordingly. Only those who must be exterminated for political reasons are exceptions to this policy. Violence forces prisoners into submission and productivity, but the real and ultimate goal is always the psychological and spiritual acquiescence of human beings.

In sum, the *Laogai* is not simply a prison system. It is a political tool for maintaining the Communist Party's totalitarian rule. The 1988 Criminal Reform Handbook of the Chinese Ministry of Justice states: "The nature of the prison as a tool of the dictatorship of classes is determined by the nature of state power." Communist Party documents clearly support forced labor in the *Laogai* to reform prisoners into "new socialist people." Thus, the Chinese Communist Party and its ideology are behind the brutal and oppressive system of the *Laogai*. Their ideas are not only different from Western concepts of freedom and reform, they are even completely antithetical to them.

TIME TO CONDEMN AND ELIMINATE THE *LAOGAI* AND THE TOTALITARIANISM IT SUPPORTS

How has Chinese history reached this sad point?

We now know that communism virtually requires human rights abuses, even though one could argue that its original intentions were good. Not so with totalitarian regimes. Sadly, Chinese communism is best described as *totalitarian* communist, with an emphasis on totalitarian. It is most like Hitler's Germany, Stalin's Russia, and Mao's China. All these systems used forced labor camps to defeat the human spirit.

Analogies to such terrorist governments are not exaggerated or radical. The Chinese Communist Party has an efficient and effective repressive machine meant to control and eliminate those it does not like. People of religious faith, political dissidents, even those who simply have a different vision of an ideal society, all have suffered and continue to suffer at the hand of Chinese communism. I estimate that 50 million Chinese have been the victims of the *Laogai* since 1949. We have identified more than 1,000 *Laogai* camps in which approximately six million people are prisoners right now.

The world eventually exposed and condemned the crimes committed by Hitler and Stalin. Yet in China, the world's most populous nation, similar human rights abuses take place today in the forced labor camps of the *Laogai*. The same Western leaders who sought to end the "Evil Empire" of the Soviet Union by calling attention to the gulag should invest similar energies in publicizing and denouncing the *Laogai*—for we will only successfully bring down the totalitarian despots in China when we deprive them of their main instruments of oppression.

We cannot honestly condemn the atrocities committed in the camps of Hitler and Stalin and continue to ignore the on-going brutality of the *Laogai*.

Chapter 9

Parental Rights are Fundamental Human Rights

Elisabeth Gusdek-Petersen

Public discussions of parental rights highlight the interaction between government and family more than most other discussions. On one side are parents, who must rear children in a given culture. On the other side is government, whose political and legal powers can change that culture.

This paper is a discussion of this interaction, and how the United Nations must recognize and respect the primacy of parents' authority to guide and protect their children.

PARENTS, THE STATE, AND THE UNITED NATIONS

As their very first responsibility, parents must provide for the physical care and protection of their children. After that, their obligation is largely two-fold: First, they must bring children to physical and psychological maturity. This manifests itself not just in

Elisabeth Gusdek-Petersen is an attorney in Switzerland specializing in family law. She has written and lectured widely on human rights and the family.

economic independence, but also in moral development (the ability of the child to acknowledge and honor obligations to others). Second (though simultaneous with the first), parents must be examples to their children, ever mindful that family influences shape a child's character more than almost anything else.

The state, whose very nature lusts for power and desires to control more and more, must be kept from trampling the integrity of the family. Indeed, the state normally need only be involved in family life to support parents. Any more direct state involvement (the displacement of parents, for example) is justified only in cases of abuse or neglect, and even then, the state should defer to other family members before assuming any direct power over children.

The United Nations knows that the state's involvement with families should be limited. Article 12 of the United Nations' Universal Declaration of Human Rights explicitly recognizes and cautions against the potential for arbitrary state interference with families. Article 16 of the Declaration also clearly establishes that the state should serve to protect the family:

> No one shall be subjected to arbitrary interference with his privacy, family, home or correspondence. ... Everyone has the right to the protection of the law against such interference or attacks.
>
> The family is the natural and fundamental group unit of society and is entitled to protection by society and the State.[1]

Similarly, Article 13 of the International Covenant on Economic, Social and Cultural Rights affirms the right of parents to choose their children's schools and moral education.[2]

All these provisions in U.N. documents acknowledge the priority of families over the state, and the primacy of parents over governments in the rearing of children. These documents have helped build a protective wall around the family, and have even encouraged the incorporation of similar measures in constitutions around the world, giving legal status to the sanctity of the family in several countries.[3] The United Nations should be commended for its contributions in this area.

THE RADICAL FEMINIST INVASION OF THE UNITED NATIONS

Unfortunately, the United Nations has not maintained its encouragement of state defense and protection of the family in recent years. It has become all too vulnerable to forces that are hostile to the family, especially the family in its traditional form of a working father and a mother who assumes primary responsibility for young children. These forces dominate the most active and influential non-governmental organizations (NGOs) at U.N. conferences and activities.[4]

Most of these NGOs subscribe to radical feminist principles, which hold that women cannot find fulfillment in child rearing and must put their own interests before those of their children. Much of this thinking is Marxist in origin and views traditional social institutions (family and church, for example) as obstacles to women's full liberation. These NGOs, therefore, seek to destroy such institutions, although they do not say this publicly. Their strategy, instead, is quietly to invade and use powerful but politically remote organizations to agitate for destruction and change. Sadly, the United Nations has proved all too easy a conquest.

Radical feminists realize that parental authority is at the heart of the traditional family. They know that if they can dismantle parental rights and responsibilities, they can bring down the entire family structure. It is no coincidence, then, that the growing influence of radical feminists within the United Nations has been accompanied by efforts there to erode parental rights and parental influence over children.

The most obvious example of these efforts is the new and fashionable campaign in favor of "children's rights," in full display in the United Nations' Convention on the Rights of the Child, approved by the United Nations General Assembly in 1989. Couched in rights rhetoric, this campaign puts traditionalists on the defensive: Few wish to oppose such efforts and be branded as anti-rights or anti-child. But the ideology that animates "rights of the child" thinking is identical to that which animates radical feminism: It is anti-family and pretends that children can exercise "rights" meaningfully so that women can be free of motherhood. This ideology is ready to sacrifice children's well-being by replacing their sanctuary, the family, with the nanny state.

One need only read Articles 12 through 16 of the U.N. Convention on the Rights of the Child to know how radical this ideology is. These

Articles confer a whole panoply of so called "rights" on children that can hardly be deemed pro-child. To start, there is free access to all media, including television, videos, Internet, computer games, and the like.[5] There is, incredibly enough, no qualification at all on content.[6] Children presumably have the "right" to view pornography. They also will presumably have "sexual rights," no doubt intended to incorporate a whole range of sexual behaviors and their consequences, including masturbation, fornication, homosexuality, etc., as well as to abortion.[7] We do not need "experts" to know that unleashing such influences on children will be devastating to their development and moral growth. Proponents of the Convention, however, seem unconcerned with this. That is, in part, why the "rights of the child" mentality is correctly called radical.[8]

It is also deemed radical because it is completely divorced from reality and from concrete experience. First, this mentality (and the documents, like the Convention, that embody it) is virtually obsessed with the concepts of autonomy and independence. Children are ostensibly encouraged to be autonomous, independent beings who simply do not need parental guidance. Indeed, this ideology deems parental authority intrusive and stifling to children and intends to emancipate them from it.

But human beings are never entirely autonomous and isolated, and children, by definition, are precisely not so. The entire process of growing up is to bring children, gradually and gently, to *relative* independence. That is, they become *less* dependent on their parents but *more depended on* by others in society, including, eventually, their own children. The radical feminist vision of the ideal human person as an isolated island free of the burdens of others is a falsehood.

Second, the autonomous, rights-bearing child is not exactly the free agent liberated from outside influences as Convention supporters would have us believe. On the contrary, the radical feminist goal is to rid children *only* of the particular influences that they cannot control, i.e., parental influence. The intention is to replace parental influence with radical feminist influence. Thus "rights of the child" talk becomes the cover for feminist indoctrination, and children become the pawns in yet another battle of our current culture war.

It goes without saying that there is no radical feminist support for parental rights. This would be antithetical to the anti-family mission. Instead, there are all sorts of emphases on women in every role but that of mother. This was clear during the Council on the Status of Women sessions held in New York in March of both 1997 and 1998. The attention of almost all the attendees was on defining papers covering such topics as "Women and the Economy," "Women in Power and Decision-Making," "Women and Migration," "Violence Against Women," etc. Women as mothers, indispensable to the development of children, did not interest them at all. Indeed, radical feminists tend to see women almost entirely as economic and political entities. If they succeed in imposing their interests, all cultural forces (legal, political and social) will favor women in these roles and not in the role of mother since the latter will simply be neglected.

WHAT MUST WE DO?

It is important to remember that the radical feminist position is a *minority* position in almost all societies, and in the first world as well as the third. (Third world women typically favor motherhood and feel that U.N. initiatives ignore their needs as mothers and their children's needs for protection and security.[9]) Supporters of the family can and should capitalize on this. Traditionalists must voice their concern over instruments such as the U.N. Convention on the Rights of the Child, and they must remain vigilant to similar types of agreements or laws in the wings.

Above all, those who recognize and wish to protect parental rights must watch initiatives and policies affecting education. There is wide consensus that parents have the basic right and responsibility to oversee their children's education, moral as well as academic. But it is in precisely this area that encroachments of parental rights will take place, since most people agree that there is a right to education (at least at the elementary level), and this usually means state-sponsored education.[10] Also, the minds of the young are malleable and vulnerable to attractive sounding notions, such as "children's rights." Parents should be on guard to reinforce and strengthen their authority in this area, legally or constitutionally, whenever they can. Only this way will they ensure a sound and healthy environment for the mental and spiritual development of their children.

This, surprisingly enough, is not always easy. Efforts to increase the state's control of education are often perceived as pro-education and pro-child. Parents themselves must expose these efforts for what they are: attempts to deprive parents of authority so that families will disintegrate and children will serve the goals of the dominant political force, and ultimately, the state.

Perhaps most importantly, parents must begin to realize how very critical they are to their children. The very presence of mothers and fathers is the best protection for children from the state, and from the misguided designs of radical feminists who would strip them of their childhood. What's more, the mother who is simply there, and the father who is involved, are the strongest influences for developing human beings.

The fact that too many parents today do not realize this, and cannot do this for their children (or are discouraged from doing so), is a great threat to children and to society. We must return to the original principles of the Universal Declaration of Human Rights and other sound U.N. documents which recognize the family's priority and the primacy of parents. Our culture must reject the nonsense of the Convention on the Rights of the Child and begin again to support parents in their guidance and education of children, allowing for state involvement only when cases of negligence warrant it. Our children depend on it.

ENDNOTES

[1] The United Nations' Universal Declaration of Human Rights, Articles 12 and 16.

[2] International Covenant on Economic, Social and Cultural Rights, Article 13, Par. 3 (1966).

[3] Including major Western European nations such as France, Germany and Austria.

[4] NGOs are organized interest groups authorized to lobby the U.N. and member nations at U.N. conferences and events.

[5] United Nations Convention on the Rights of the Child, Article 13, Par. 1 (1989): "The child shall have the right to freedom of expression; **this right shall include freedom to seek, receive, and impart information and ideas of all kinds, regardless of frontiers,** either orally, in writing or in print, in the form of art, or **through any other media of the child's choice.**" (emphasis added)

[6] The Convention only allows limitations that are "necessary," the interpretation of which is exceedingly unclear.

[7] Article 16 of the Convention confers a right of privacy on children. In the United States, many courts construe the right to privacy to include the "right" to sexual activity and abortion.

[8] It should also be said that promotion of rights-of-the-child thinking comes primarily from the first world countries, such as the United States and Canada, to the dismay of third world peoples. The latter often feel that the real problems for them and for their children concern security and stability in the home and protection, especially in areas dominated by armed conflict. See, for example, Statement, Olara A. Otunnu, Under-Secretary-General at the United Nations, Representative for Children in Armed Conflict, *To Strengthen the Family*, Human Rights Conference in Geneva, 20 April 1998.

[9] *Id.*

[10] The United Nations' Universal Declaration of Human Rights, Article 26.

Chapter 10

The Wrongs of the United Nations' Rights of the Child

Charles Francis

After World War II, when the United Nations first became established, most people looked to it with hope for the future. Primarily it was envisaged as a world authority, which would serve to prevent wars and act as mediator and arbitrator when disputes developed between member nations. Secondly, as the gross violations of human rights by the Nazi regime became more fully known, the United Nations was seen also as a world body to establish and protect human rights throughout the world.

This essay discusses human rights in the context of the present "rights of the child" mentality prevailing at the United Nations. Legitimate concern for the world's children has, unfortunately, given way to a dangerous and false vision of an autonomous child with the same objectionable humanist "rights" as any adult. This vision, if given legal effect or legitimacy of any kind, poses a real threat to the authority of parents and to the integrity of the family.

Charles H. Francis is an attorney in Toorak, Victoria, Australia. He has written widely on human rights and legal history.

IN THE BEGINNING: CHRISTIAN INFLUENCE AT THE UNITED NATIONS AND THE BEST INTERESTS OF CHILDREN

Most of the countries that played a major part in the early development of the United Nations and in the drafting of its first declarations had a strong underlying Christian and thus pro-family ethos.[1] The Universal Declaration of Human Rights, adopted by the General Assembly fifty years ago, is evidence of this, asserting, as it does, "Motherhood and childhood are entitled to special care and assistance," in Article 25(2), and declaring, "Parents have a prior right to choose the kind of education that shall be given to their children," in Article 26(3). The United Nations made similar declarations after this that tended to focus on improving children's health, nutrition, safety, and education.[2] There appeared to be a general agreement that such interests were ordinarily best served by keeping children within integrated families and under the care, guidance and control of their parents.

THE TURN TO HUMANISM AND TO DELIBERATE AMBIGUITY

In 1989, the United Nations General Assembly introduced a new Convention on the Rights of the Child. It was promptly signed by 130 nations with, it would seem, singularly little debate or scrutiny and even less intelligent discussion on the legal effect of its provisions.

This Convention was full of platitudinous phrases and contained much ambiguous language. However, many prominent lawyers became aware of the problems and traps within it and lectured and wrote on its proper interpretation, warning their countries not to sign or ratify it. Most of the representatives of the various nations, which rushed like so many lemmings to sign the Convention, probably had no real understanding of its meaning. It was feted as a Convention in the best interests of children, and those nations that signed it were said to demonstrate a commitment to the prevention of child abuse. Those who expressed concern about possible interpretations of the Convention were falsely assured that parental rights were fully preserved by Article Five.[3]

A number of the supporters of this 1989 Children's Rights Convention also maintained, quite falsely, that its main object was the protection of children, and that it did no more than provide for those rights that were already law in more advanced democracies such as the

United States of America. In reality, had legislation setting out similar provisions to those of the Convention been introduced into the House of Representatives in the United States (or in Australia), it would probably never have become law.[4]

By 1989, however, many supporters of humanist philosophies had already realized it was far easier to implement their ideas by incorporating them in United Nations' Conventions, which their countries might thereafter ratify, rather than by attempting the more difficult (if not impossible) task of trying to pass such provisions through their countries' legislatures, where they were likely to receive much closer scrutiny, and where the legal interpretation and actual effect of the provisions might be the subject of proper analysis and debate.[5]

In essence, the 1989 Children's Rights Convention was humanist (*not* Christian). Humanism denies and rejects God (as well as prayer, any divine purpose and theism generally) and all religions that place God above human desires. Despite its followers' claims of neutrality, humanism is a secular religion, and is more dogmatic than any church teaching. Humanism recognizes and accepts abortion, euthanasia, suicide and countless other immoral acts, and works for the establishment of a completely secular society, which is its goal. It also realizes that the traditional family, marked by strong parental authority, is an obstacle to this goal and, therefore, seeks to dismantle it.

In consequence, the 1989 Convention gave to children a sphere of autonomy and freedom from control (in particular a freedom from parental control) and thereby introduced a radically new concept of children having rights entirely separate from their parents, with the government accepting the responsibility for protecting the child from the power of parents.

Professor Bruce Hafen of Brigham Young University has wisely pointed out that parents who subscribe to "children's rights" thinking and "leave their children alone" so they develop their personalities are irresponsibly abrogating their parental duties, leaving their children a ready prey to a wide range of immoral and evil influences.[6] Indeed, in England some of the strongest support for "children's rights" has come from well identified homosexual and pedophile organizations, which long ago realized that the easiest way to obtain access to children was to demand their freedom from any form of restraint, thereby exposing them to the predatory behavior of those who would harm them.[7]

While some Articles of the Convention are praiseworthy (for example, its prohibitions on slavery and child prostitution), there are five Articles in particular (12, 13, 14, 15 and 16, discussed below) that would create grave difficulties for parents seeking to exercise authority over children. These Articles appear to be the spearhead of a very serious invasion of parental rights.

ARTICLES 12 TO 16

Article 12 is the first to provide a charter of autonomous children's rights. Its implications therefore require close attention. It assures to a child the right to express views freely in all matters affecting the child, the view of the child being given due weight in accordance with the age and maturity of the child.

But who is to determine what weight is to be attached to those views? Obviously not the parents alone. Article 12 enables children to ventilate their disagreements with parental rulings in primarily public and legal forums.[8] Carried to its logical conclusion, the child will be able to demand state intervention to challenge any parental conduct the child doesn't like (or conduct the child claims is not in his "best interest"). This is an absurd threat to parental authority.

Article 13 assures to the child the right of freedom of expression, which includes "freedom to seek, receive and impart information and ideas of all kinds." This Article will prevent parents from protecting their children from objectionable or immoral materials, often disseminated in schools. A recent case in Australia provides a most disturbing example: When a family tried to persuade their daughter's school that some of its curriculum was inappropriate for young secondary students, the Department of Secondary Education invoked the provisions of the Convention as authority for overriding parental rights and wishes.[9]

We would do well, at this juncture, to consider some material that the United Nations has already approved for children, since we can assume that the Convention on the Rights of the Child would support the unrestricted dissemination of such material to them.

The United Nations Children's Fund (UNICEF) has already produced two sex education films, "The Blue Pigeon" and "Music for Two." "The Blue Pigeon" is a cartoon targeted at 10- to 12- year-old children, and graphically depicts sexual intercourse between two children attending a children's picnic. "Music for Two" depicts the fantasies of a young girl who foresees herself as tired, overworked and overburdened when married, and her husband as indifferent and uninterested. By contrast, sexual intercourse with a boy neighbor is depicted as a happy, commitment-free sexual relationship.[10]

It takes no genius to discern this message of approval for sexual activity outside of marriage and even for children at a very young age. Parents must understand that this is the type of "information" the United Nations wishes to "impart" to their children.

Article 14 declares "the right of the child to freedom of thought, conscience and religion." The Convention affords parents and guardians only the limited right to "direct" children in the exercise of this right (although there is no real protection for this right; the state merely gives it "respect," which, without means of enforcement, is somewhat meaningless). "Direction" of course implies that a parent will not be able to *require* a young child to go to church or Sunday school if the child does not wish to do so.[11]

American Christian leader Dr. James Dobson has suggested that the real freedom given by Article 14 is freedom from parental control in the area of religion. Parents are relegated to providing a state-monitored influence over the religious practices of their own children.[12]

Article 15 "recognizes" the right of the child to freedom of association and the right to freedom of peaceful assembly. Such rights make it difficult, if not impossible, for parents to control the company their children keep, even though that company may be truly harmful. The Convention does not balance these "children's rights" against those of parents (which should always serve the best interests of children), however valid and compelling. In some Australian towns where young teenage vandalism and crime is rife, teenage curfews have been introduced. Usually they have proved successful, but civil libertarians have already complained that curfews are a breach of Article 15 of the Convention. In this regard, the Convention appears to be directly opposed to the view of the United States Supreme Court, which has held such curfews lawful.[13]

Article 16 protects the child's right not to be "subjected to arbitrary or unlawful interference with his or her privacy." The inclusion of the word *arbitrary* may permit children to exclude parents from anything they consider private, including medical treatments, and presumably activity in the child's bedroom or any other part of the home set aside for the child's use. This Article greatly strengthens the position of Planned Parenthood, which routinely puts young girls on birth control pills without notice to (much less consent from) their parents. The United States Supreme Court has, of course, already upheld privacy rights for children in the context of abortion and contraception. Mature minors (maturity being determined by a judge) can have abortions without any parental involvement, and immature minors may have abortions if the judge thinks it is in their best interests.

THE NEED TO COMBAT THE UNITED NATIONS' "RIGHTS OF THE CHILD"

The picture should be clear by now: The Convention is a very serious invasion of parental rights. A careful analysis of its terms proves that it is anti-parent. It takes many important decisions regarding the well-being of children (on education, philosophy, morality and religion) away from parents and gives them to the State, and ultimately, to the United Nations itself.

Most great civilizations have been destroyed not from without but from within. In almost every such instance, the breakdown of the family was key to the collapse. Responsible parents realize that children (especially adolescent children) need protection from their own actions which spring from a lack of mature judgment. The Convention's invasion of parental control can only make this task more difficult, if not impossible.

The new humanist philosophy, increasingly embraced by so many Western democracies today, and brought to the United Nations by their delegates, has enormous potential for harm, especially when applied to our children. The U.N. Convention on the Rights of the Child reflects this philosophy and is, in many ways, diametrically opposed to what the United Nations had to offer the world in its 1948 Universal Declaration of Human Rights.

We desperately need to re-appraise the United Nations' present direction. We must realize that those humanist philosophies, which masquerade as a concern for human rights, will end up trampling them —just as the United Nations' Convention on the Rights of the Child pretends to protect children but damages the parental authority that is their best protection. The humanist element of such documents has the potential to destroy all that is best in Christian civilization, replacing it with a profoundly chaotic, harmful and ultimately evil empire.

ENDNOTES

[1] The United States and Great Britain were foremost among them. To some extent, the drafters of the postwar declarations were using 20th-century national constitutions as their models, adding the protection of the family and the child to those political and civil democratic rights that they wished to identify and preserve.

[2] Such declarations included the Declaration of the Rights of the Child in 1959, a valuable document that included Principle 6, providing that "the child shall wherever possible grow up in the care and under the responsibility of his parents." The 1959 Declaration was in many ways not unlike the 1924 League of Nations Declaration on the Rights of the Child, which had stated that "mankind owes to the child the best it has to give." The philosophy of the 1959 Declaration was again essentially Christian, and anticipated that, at a later date, there would be further and more detailed provisions.

[3] Article 5 reads as follows: "States Parties shall respect the responsibilities, rights, and duties of parents or, where applicable, the members of the extended family or community as provided for by local custom, legal guardians or other persons legally responsible for the child, to provide, in a manner consistent with the evolving capacities of the child, appropriate direction and guidance in the exercise by the child of the rights recognized in the present Convention."

But who is to decide what constitutes "a manner consistent with the evolving capacities of the child"? When this Article is read in conjunction with the child's rights contained in Articles 12 to 16, and with the fact that parents have no right of control, it is apparent that this determination is not necessarily to be left to the parents alone.

[4] The obvious legal implications of Articles 12 to 16, once properly understood and publicized (as they were in the U.S. Senate), are likely to lead to their rejection. (In Australia, the adoption of these Articles as Federal law would necessitate an amendment to the Constitution by referendum.)

[5] In England, however, some unfortunate features similar to those of the Convention found their way into the *Child Act* of 1989.

[6] Professor Bruce C. Hafen, and Jonathan O. Hafen (1996) *Harvard International Law Journal* 37(2), pp. 449-491.

[7] See "The Fight for the Family" 1998, Lynette Burrows, Family Education Trust, Oxford, England, ISBN 0 906229 14 6.

[8] Article 12(2) reads: "[T]he child shall in particular be provided the opportunity to be heard in any judicial and administrative proceedings affecting the child, either directly, or through a representative or an appropriate body, in a manner consistent with the procedural rules of national law."

[9] *Newsweekly* (Australia) January 24, 1998, at 17. The U.N. has a track record in this regard: Its Committee on the Rights of the Child has already criticized England for not having a way for children to dissent from parental views. The Committee's criticism was made in relation to parents withdrawing their

children from school sex education programs that the parents deemed unsuitable. U.N. Committee on the Rights of the Child, Report on the United Kingdom, February 15, 1995.

[10] "Behind the Mask of UNICEF," *Population Research Institute Review* (1992), Baltimore, MD.

[11] Professor Bruce Hafen, when speaking in Ireland last year, confirmed this interpretation of Article 14 when he said that a parent who might compel his child to go to Mass could well find himself in breach of this Article. *The Irish News*, March 26, 1997.

[12] Satanic cults will no doubt make use (or misuse) of Article 14, which enables them to attract children away from the religions of their families more easily. Such cults are typically interested in young children or adolescents.

[13] *City of Dallas v. Stenglin*, 490 US 19 (1989).

Chapter 11

Publicly Funded Schools: The United Nations' Captive Audience

Nick Seaton

In Great Britain, the United Nations (U.N.) is like Mother's apple pie: Almost everyone loves and respects it, and hesitates to criticize it. The United Nations' Universal Declaration of Human Rights also enjoys respect and popularity, providing as it does guiding principles for any liberal-democratic nation state.

The Universal Declaration addresses the topic of education in a number of areas. The most explicit reference is in Article 26, which reads, in part: (1) *Everyone has the right to education.*[1] (2) *Education shall be directed toward the full development of the human personality and to the strengthening of respect for human rights and fundamental freedoms.*[2] (3) *Parents have a prior right to choose the kind of education that shall be given to their children.*

The reference to parents is especially significant, since it

Nick Seaton is an experienced school governor and chairman of the Campaign for Real Education, which seeks to raise standards and improve choice in state education. He is author of the recently-published New Gods for Schools: Self, Society, Relationships and the Environment *(CRE, 1998).*

acknowledges the primacy of the family in educational matters. The Declaration recognizes elsewhere the family's importance, declaring in Article 16: "The family is the natural and fundamental group unit of society and is entitled to protection by society and by the State."[3]

Given the above, it seems fair to assume that the United Nations originally understood the need to support parents in their efforts to educate children, since this was primarily a parental responsibility.

Unfortunately, however, the United Nations has departed from these principles. Despite its continued apple-pie reputation, the United Nations (and the non-governmental organizations (NGOs) that influence it) is compromising these principles with educational programs hostile to parental authority and the traditions most parents favor. The United Nations now represents an educational philosophy quite different from the one envisaged by Articles 16 and 26. This essay describes that philosophy and shows how its values systematically undermine the traditional family and religious faith.

COMPETING EDUCATIONAL PHILOSOPHIES

To understand the world of education at the primary and secondary level, one must first appreciate the two contradictory philosophies that are competing for supremacy there.

First is the traditional philosophy of education. It maintains that children attend school to learn the content and facts of a structured, subject-centered curriculum. For example, it requires that pupils learn multiplication tables, correct spelling, standard grammar, dates of historical events, and the like. Knowledge, accuracy and analysis are important. Objective examinations then test the amount learned.

Traditional education tends to be authoritarian and hierarchical. It is certainly disciplined, to create the conditions necessary for concentration and learning.

Concepts of right and wrong underpin traditional education for both academics and morals. Academically speaking, students either have factual knowledge or they do not. With respect to moral education, teachers and parents teach values both by example (for punctuality, industriousness, self-discipline, honesty, and so on) and by instruction (religion can be a component of the curriculum, for example). Rules themselves, of course, teach and reinforce the notion that there is a right and wrong.

Traditional education accepts competition as a necessary part of life and welcomes the good it can produce (competition can motivate students to learn lessons better, for example). Traditionalists also acknowledge that children have varying abilities and aptitudes. They see this variety as a challenge to find different gifts among students. Such differences guide choices, made with parents, about schools, courses and extracurricular activities for any given pupil.

In contrast to this is the modern philosophy which holds that education should be child-centered and "relevant." Skills take precedence over knowledge (for example, "learning how to learn"), and problem solving replaces teaching—indeed, instructors are called "facilitators," not teachers. Exploration of feelings and "understanding" are more important than facts, which, modernists contend, are relative anyway. Self-image, self-esteem and relationships matter more than performance, just as the process is more important than the product.[4] Cooperation among and within groups is preferred to competition, and subjective values replace objective virtue. Of these values, egalitarianism is paramount, requiring that, wherever possible, equality of result displace equality of opportunity.

THE PURPOSE OF EDUCATION

Most important is the disagreement between these two philosophies about the fundamental purpose of education. Traditionalists believe that education should improve the individual and, indirectly, the family. The goal is both academic and moral and tends to stabilize society. Progressives, on the other hand, believe that the purpose of education is to change society. They by definition dislike tradition and stability. Thus, theirs is primarily a political goal with destabilizing effects.

While the traditionalist seeks to transfer a body of knowledge and time-tested values to future generations, the progressive replaces tradition and parental guidance with choices for the child. Progressives encourage each child to teach himself and to learn academics and morals from his peers. They deem any attempt to transfer values from adults (parents or teachers) to children as "indoctrination," not education.

At root, the progressive approach to education rejects the truth and the God that our Western Judeo-Christian tradition has tried to serve.

The majority of parents, Christian and non-Christian, favor this tradition (even though it can feel burdensome), since it demands that human conduct conform to objective moral norms. Progressives prefer the individual as creator and arbiter of right and wrong, which boils down to doing what one wants, or selfishness dressed up as "enlightened morality." When there is an objective moral order (a right and wrong that exist outside ourselves), we must conform our behavior to it, which is much less convenient.

Progressives did not want, however, to discard the idea of moral authority that accompanied the Judeo-Christian tradition. Thus, they kept its form and gutted its substance: They replaced objectivity and truth with individual subjectivity in the realms of both factual knowledge and morality. In this way they could retain moral credibility while ridding themselves of onerous behavioral constraints.

PERSONAL, SOCIAL AND HEALTH EDUCATION (PSHE) TO REPLACE RELIGION

The attempt to replace the old morality with a more "enlightened" (read permissive) new one is most evident in the efforts to replace Religious Education with what is called "Personal, Social and Health Education," or PSHE. Since 1988 (when England and Wales approved a statutory National Curriculum consisting of 10 subjects plus Religious Education, or "RE," which includes statutory daily worship), progressives have tried *twice* to replace RE with PSHE and have made aggressive efforts to integrate PSHE into all subjects. This integration (teaching PSHE within another subject so that all subjects must include PSHE elements) serves three purposes. First, it reduces the time available to teach factual knowledge. Second, it politicizes all subjects (history, for example, can be devoted to "gender" and other issues). Third, and perhaps most important, it makes it impossible for parents to withdraw their child from PSHE (to be contrasted with the specific parental right to withdraw their children from RE and worship). In this way progressives impose their moral view on all students.

In Britain, the chief executive of the Curriculum and Qualifications Authority (a progressive NGO that has changed its name three times since its beginning), Dr. Nick Tate, is leading the latest effort to make PSHE a compulsory program. This time, he will almost certainly succeed. He began by forming a "National Forum for Values in

Education and the Community," with 150 members—almost all of the progressive ilk. Once the Forum had specified its "common values" under four headings—self, society, relationships, and the environment—it was disbanded, to be replaced by yet another 50-strong group. This group (also dominated by progressives) was charged with providing guidance for schools based on the original Forum's "common values," which were cross-referenced with "spiritual, moral and social development." But despite protests from the few traditionalists present, religion was specifically excluded from spiritual development!

It cannot be over-emphasized that PSHE is a religion substitute: In place of religious faith and instruction, secular progressives offer "personal health," "social values" and the like. At the same time, paradoxically, however, their new morality is more dogmatic than traditional religious faiths, since it is not recognized as a religion and people cannot "opt out" of its demands as they can with instruction in other confessions.[5]

Thus, progressives not only claim a new and better morality than that of supposedly unenlightened traditionalists; they also position themselves to impose it on others without limitation and without allowing them any choice. It is no coincidence that the United Nations human rights documents have become favorite tools among PSHE advocates. Once their values are recognized as "human rights," progressives will demand that everyone observe them as universal "rights," above and beyond local cultures and even above and beyond national laws.[6]

THE U.N.'S PROMOTION OF NEW "GLOBAL" VALUES

These PSHE proposals will almost certainly become law in England and Wales by the year 2000, when an updated version of the National Curriculum is scheduled to take effect. But even absent statutory approval, the progressive philosophy has become standard educational fare in most of the major democracies.[7]

Yet similarities in content and enforcement of educational reform could not simply occur without some guiding force. Nor is it likely to be coincidental that the new "core" values planned for English state schools are almost identical to those recommended by the United Nations' Commission on Global Governance in its 1995 report, *Our*

Global Neighbourhood.[8] *Our Global Neighbourhood* calls for the promotion of "global values," which are "core values that can unite people of all cultural, political, religious, or philosophical backgrounds [sic]."[9] While this report pays lip service to traditional religions, national sovereignty, national self-determination, parliamentary democracy and private property rights, its overall thrust is toward a form of international socialism, based on "quality of life," "relationships," and "responsibility for the global neighbourhood."[10]

The U.N. clearly intends education to be a primary vehicle for advancing these values worldwide. Indeed, a document published by UNESCO in 1978 describes "the school with its captive audience" as "an obvious place" to promote progressive ideology, thus avoiding any need to overcome "deeply entrenched traditional learning."[11] A senior U.N. official, Robert Muller, followed the same ideological line in his influential book, *New Genesis: Shaping a Global Spirituality*, published in 1982. Muller called for a "world core curriculum aimed at all levels, grades and forms of education."[12] He also wrote approvingly of "those for whom the United Nations is a new form of spirituality and ethics," noting that the U.N. has become "holy ground" where people find inspiration as "world servants."[13]

VALUES CLARIFICATION, NOT VALUES TRANSFERENCE

A key weapon in the progressive armory, also favored by U.N. acolytes, is the psychological technique known as values clarification.[14] Now widely practiced in values education lessons, values clarification is the antithesis of traditional values transference and clear evidence of the progressive philosophy at work. Jim Bowen, a Melbourne barrister and president of the Victorian chapter of the Australian Family Association, explains:

> The core theme of values clarification is that ... there are no right or wrong values. Values clarification does not seek to identify and transmit 'right' values, but to help children to discover the values that best suit them personally in a particular situation. ... Children are subjected [in the classroom] to searching questions about personal and family beliefs, attitudes and behavior. ... In a context resembling group therapy ... tools, such as sensitivity training, are employed to produce changes in children's attitudes and behavior. In role playing games, children are subjected to mental stress. ... Doubts concerning

previously held values and loyalties are implanted ... leaving them open to implantation of other values.[15]

In brief, so-called "values clarification" is a way to disabuse children of traditional morals. Role-playing teaches them that objective moral norms may make some people feel bad. These feelings are then presumed to be evidence of the invalidity of such norms.

This results, predictably, in moral relativism. Practically speaking, it leaves children without any moral guidance, and invites them to make choices based on their feelings. Peer pressure becomes more powerful, and behavior sinks to the lowest common denominator.[16] This is obviously dangerous for impressionable children.

Indeed, noted pioneers of values clarification have become concerned about its dangerous effects, and, in fact, one of them works full-time to expose its risks. Describing how values clarification had destroyed Catholic orders in America, Dr. William Coulson said, "There were some 600 nuns when we began. Within a year after our first interventions, 300 of them were petitioning Rome to get out of their vows. They did not want to be under anyone's authority, except the authority of their imperial inner selves."[17] If these techniques can so easily undermine the morality of adult nuns, what are the prospects for young and immature students?

KNOWING THE BUZZ WORDS AND WHERE TO GO FROM HERE

Progressives have deliberately confused many parents and teachers.[18] To respond, responsible adults must inform and organize themselves to defend their families and their children. All adults should recognize that the following are progressive inventions to undermine traditional education: global education; outcome-based education; citizenship education; environmental education; health education; population education; sex education (in schools instead of in families); most drug education; life-skills; personal development; and self-esteem programs. All of these inventions rely on values clarification, and all turn teachers into untrained psychologists and social workers. Most important, all seek to replace religious and family values with humanistic secular and subjective values.

The dominance of the progressive ideology in our primary and secondary schools amounts to a challenge to parents: U.N.-style education reform is a direct challenge to parental authority and to the tradition that has served families so well for so long.[19] But it is also a challenge to parents to reclaim their rights over children pursuant to the United Nations' own Universal Declaration of Human Rights. Parents simply must meet this challenge head-on and insist upon their rightful place in the education of their children.

Indeed, the well-being of our young depends on it.

ENDNOTES

[1] The remainder of the paragraph reads: *Education shall be free, at least in the elementary and fundamental stages. Elementary education shall be compulsory. Technical and professional education shall be made generally available and higher education shall be equally accessible to all on the basis of merit.* United Nations, Universal Declaration of Human Rights (1948), Article 26 (1).

[2] *Ibid.*, Article 26 (2). The remainder of the paragraph reads: *It [education] shall promote understanding, tolerance, and friendship among all nations, racial or religious groups* [sic]*, and shall further the activities of the United Nations for the maintenance of peace.*

[3] *Ibid.*, Article 16 (3).

[4] *See* Marilyn Ferguson, *The Aquarian Conspiracy: Personal and Social Transformation in the 1980s* (London: Routledge & Kegan Paul, 1982).

[5] This "new morality" relies heavily on New Ageism (the universal replacement for traditional religions) and draws on totalitarian ideologies such as Marxism (International Socialism) and Fascism (National Socialism). *See*, for example, J. Noakes and G. Pridham, Eds., *Nazism 1919-1945: State, Economy and Society 1933-1939* (Exeter: University of Exeter, 1984).

[6] This is, after all, the essence of "human rights," properly speaking: They are before and above any nation state and its laws.

[7] Literature from Australia, New Zealand, Canada, France, Switzerland, Ireland and the United Kingdom shows considerable similarities among the progressive programs being introduced in all these countries. *See* for example *OQE Forum*, the newsletters of the Organisation for Quality Education, based in Waterloo, Ontario, Canada, and *Education or Manipulation: What's Going on in Irish Schools Today* (Cork: Irish Educational Research, 1995).

[8] Report of the Commission on Global Governance, *Our Global Neighbourhood* (New York: Oxford University Press, 1995), p. 48.

[9] *Ibid.*

[10] *Ibid.*

[11] "Population Education: A Contemporary Concern" (UNESCO, 1978), p. 25. This is No. 28 of a series of Educational Studies and Documents published by UNESCO.

[12] Robert Muller, *New Genesis: Shaping a Global Spirituality* (Garden City, N.Y.: Doubleday & Company, Inc., 1982), p. 140.

[13] *Ibid.*, p. 46.

[14] *See* Carl Rogers, *Freedom To Learn for the 80s* (Columbus: Charles E. Merrill Publishing Company, 1983), the seminal work on values clarification, of which Rogers was a pioneer. (Rogers's books are recommended in *Group techniques in education,* No. 24 in a series of "educational studies and documents" published by UNESCO, date unknown.)

[15] Jim Bowen, "Why classrooms have become a battleground," *News Weekly,* March 3, 1990.

[16] It should, perhaps, be noted here that the techniques used in "circle time" are similar to those used in values clarification—and they share the same objectives. *See* Jenny Mosley, *Quality Circle Time in the Primary Classroom* (Wisbech, Cambridgeshire: LDA, 1996.)

[17] Interview with Dr. William Coulson, "We overcame their traditions, we overcame their faith," *The Latin Mass,* January-February, 1994.

[18] *See* Antony Flew and Fred Naylor, *Spiritual Development and All That Jazz,* (York: Campaign for Real Education, 1997).

[19] It is also a challenge to politicians, who husband taxpayer money. Without these funds, organizations such as the United Nations would be forced to concentrate on their primary purpose—in this case, the honest protection of human rights rather than the destruction of traditional families and religion.

Chapter 12

The International Criminal Court, Human Rights and the Family

Richard G. Wilkins and Kathryn O. Balmforth

One hundred and twenty countries voted in Rome, Italy, in July 1998 to create a permanent International Criminal Court (ICC). The vote was the result of a decades-long effort by the United Nations and the international community to establish a permanent (and powerful) world criminal court. Although the new court ostensibly is designed to deal only with the "most serious crimes of international concern,"[1] it has a broad "human rights" reach, which means it may well intrude upon traditional cultural and religious norms—particularly those involving the family.

Continued vigilance in monitoring the developing ICC (like that exhibited by a family values coalition that attended the Rome conference) will be vitally important.

Richard G. Wilkins is a professor of law at Brigham Young University and director of Family Voice, a non-governmental organization. Kathryn O. Balmforth is executive director and legal counsel for Family Voice.

THE IMPETUS FOR THE ICC

In 1945, following the conclusion of the Nuremberg and Tokyo War Crime Tribunals, a proposal was circulated among members of the newly formed United Nations to create a permanent standing court.[2] The proposed court was to be responsible for prosecuting grave crimes committed in armed conflict. The nations of the world initially balked at the idea of a permanent court because of the possible compromise to individual state sovereignty.[3] The idea, however, continued to resurface whenever the world was confronted with serious wartime crimes.

Finally, at the conclusion of the Iran-Iraq War in December 1989, the General Assembly of the United Nations passed a resolution calling for the official creation of a permanent criminal court to deal with war-related atrocities.[4] Public pressure for the creation of this court, as the world reacted to reported atrocities in Rwanda and the former Yugoslavia, was a major factor at this time. Informal meetings on the issue commenced early in 1990 and ultimately resulted in a draft statute for the ICC.

As that draft statute emerged, however, the mandate for the proposed ICC slowly but steadily expanded. Instead of dealing solely with serious and well established war crimes, the draft text became a veritable handbook on emerging "human rights" law, weighted with countless provisions never envisioned by the General Assembly's initial resolution supporting the ICC. This complex and convoluted draft statute was presented to U.N. delegates at Rome during the summer of 1998 for finalization.[5]

THE POSSIBLE DANGERS OF THE ICC

The draft ICC statute condemned "war crimes" and "crimes against humanity"[6]—abstract condemnations that, on the surface, are quite laudable. The world unquestionably would be a better place without "war crimes" and "crimes against humanity." The devil, of course, is in the details. Some of the "details" provided by the draft statute were decidedly worrisome.

As a briefing paper prepared for the Rome ICC conference by non-governmental organization Family Voice (a family values organization sponsored by Brigham Young University) pointed out:

> The vaguely worded "crimes" created by the [draft] ICC, including the "war crime" of "enforced pregnancy" and the "crime against humanity" of

"persecution," pose serious risks of condemning (and eliminating) traditional cultural and religious values. Among other things, [the "crime" of "enforced pregnancy" could mandate abortion on demand, while] the crime of "persecution" could be used to criminalize denial of homosexual marriage and outlaw all religious practices that differentiate between men and women.[7]

The ultimate aim envisioned by those who championed the inclusion of these "crimes" in the draft was straightforward: They sought to empower the new international court to undertake a thorough judicial revision of basic societal norms.

Two years of consistent attendance and participation at numerous U.N. meetings and conferences has persuaded us that many purported international policy experts (and, disquietingly, national delegations) within the U.N. system are thoroughly anti-religion and anti-family. Motherhood, rather than being celebrated, is portrayed as an odious social "stereotype" which interferes with women's preferred role as paid workers.[8] Marriage is seldom if ever discussed in positive terms. It is routinely portrayed as an oppressive, anti-woman regime.[9] Abortion is consistently promoted, despite the fact that consensus has never been reached on a right to abortion.[10] Children are unfortunate burdens that can and should be prevented by proper medical care[11] but who, if prevention fails, must be trained free of "undue" parental control and without the "prejudices" inculcated by traditional culture and religion.[12] Homosexuality is to be normalized and protected from "discrimination."[13]

THE RESPONSE

The draft language of the ICC statute was ominous. It suggested (among other things) that judges should be empowered to condemn "enforced pregnancy" and "gender-based persecution" because global society has not yet accepted abortion on demand and same-sex "marriage." Fortunately, these immediate possible consequences are somewhat less likely because of the efforts of a coalition of non-governmental organizations (NGOs) committed to the preservation of traditional values.[14]

The thrust of the proposed "crime" of "enforced pregnancy" was clear: Any legal regime that forbade termination of unwanted pregnancies would be guilty of "enforced pregnancy."[15] The pro-family coalition argued that, while rape or sexual violence properly should be condemned, the status of "pregnancy" should not be criminalized. While rape or other sexual misconduct that could result in pregnancy might properly be considered criminal, it is straining the bounds of logic to assert that pregnancy (in any circumstance) is itself a "crime." Far from constituting a "crime against humanity," pregnancy is the necessary precondition to continuation of humanity itself.

The coalition also argued for straightforward usage of the term *gender*.[16] *Gender*—in ordinary usage—brings to mind typical notions of *male* and *female*. Indeed, the French and Arabic versions of the draft statute referred to "the two sexes" rather than *gender*. In English, however, ICC scriveners used *gender*—an unfortunately ambiguous word hardly limited, in this context, to "the two sexes."[17] In fact, because of the contentious nature of the arguments surrounding *gender*, the word had never been defined in *any* binding U.N. document prior to the conclusion of the ICC conference.

The ICC conference did not adopt the unrestrained "crime" of "enforced pregnancy," nor did it create new and wide-ranging "gender" rights. Instead, the final ICC statute criminalizes "the unlawful confinement of a woman forcibly made pregnant, with the intent of affecting the ethnic composition of any population or carrying out other grave violations of international law."[18] *Gender*, furthermore, was defined as "the two sexes, male and female, within the context of society. The term gender does not mean anything different than this."[19] These significant alterations in the statute, while not made without difficulties,[20] represent important advances for the proponents of traditional values at the United Nations.

Although pregnancy in limited circumstances is now (for the first time) criminal, the proscribed criminal conduct is narrowly defined. As defined, "forced pregnancy" does not (as its supporters had hoped) establish an international legal regime in which "abortion is essential to women's full personhood."[21] On the contrary, the ICC establishes criminal liability only when a woman is unlawfully detained and forcibly made pregnant with criminal intent. *Gender*, furthermore, does *not* mean everything (i.e., all sexuality from hetero- to homo- to bi- and beyond) and nothing (i.e., not "male" or "female"). On the contrary, *gender* means "male and female" in "the context of society" and "does not indicate any [different] meaning."[22] This definition represents a significant departure from prior U.N. usage, which has repeatedly asserted that gender is a mere "social construct" not tied to "immutable biological differences."[23]

The process that resulted in these changes was hardly orderly—or even fair. For example, when debate at the Rome conference indicated that many nations strongly supported *deletion* of the "crime" of "enforced pregnancy," the chair suspended discussion. Thereafter, Canada, with enthusiastic support from the European Union, convened a secret meeting on Sunday, July 5, where a hand-picked group of predictably supportive states met to hammer out a "consensus" which (not surprisingly) continued to condemn "forced" pregnancy.[24] A similar process, involving the closure of public debate after a Canadian representative asserted that international failure to recognize same-sex marriage could only be explained on the grounds of mere "bigotry," was repeated on the "gender" issue. Despite all this—the closure of debate, the initiation of secret meetings, and subsequent resolution through non-public "back room" compromises—the family values coalition was able to obtain a satisfactory outcome on these important matters.

Maintaining that satisfactory outcome will be the real challenge.

THE FUTURE

At 11:00 p.m. on July 17, 1998, the international community voted to adopt the ICC statute. A strong family values coalition participated in the Rome conference and provided the impetus for important alterations of the proposed ICC statute.

While the coalition scored substantial "victories" in preventing abortion on demand and defining *gender*, the final vote adopting the ICC statute remains an intensely sobering event. The *Rome Statute of the International Criminal Court* represents a remarkable expansion of international power over sensitive moral questions that sovereign states traditionally have addressed. Its approval signals a new era in which international institutions successfully attempt to displace sovereign nations.

This development imposes a substantial obligation on citizens who support traditional values, including the value of self-government in nation states. The ICC threatens all of this. Its supporters, though ultimately unsuccessful, did *try* to draft the ICC statute even more radically, hoping to "cast aside millennia of moral teaching."[25] These supporters will likely multiply and grow stronger following the conclusion of the Rome ICC conference. There are, for example, well-organized movements within the United Nations system that hope to "reinterpret" basic human rights documents. Such "reinterpretation" means creating such "fundamental rights" as abortion on demand and freedom from "discrimination based on sexual orientation," as well as condemning the "stereotype" of motherhood.[26] The documents to be "reinterpreted" include the International Covenant on Civil and Political Rights and the Universal Declaration of Human Rights.

Citizens from all nations who believe in the sanctity of life, the centrality of traditional family structure, and the preservation of long-standing cultural values must make their voices heard to defeat this anti-family effort. Raising that voice, as any member of the family values coalition at the Rome conference could testify, can be unpleasant. But, as the Rome conference also demonstrates, world leaders (particularly from developing countries) will not only listen—they will be grateful to hear family proponents speak. It may be difficult, but the importance of the task forbids silence.

ENDNOTES

[1] *Rome Statute of the International Criminal Court*, U.N. ICC, Rome, 1998, Art. 5 & 1, at 4 (U.N. Doc. A/Conf.183/9).

[2] Benjamin B. Ferencz, *International Criminal Courts: The Legacy of Nuremberg*, 10 Pace Int'l L. Rev., 1998.

[3] *Ibid.*

[4] *Establishment of an International Criminal Court*, at <gopher://gopher.un.org/00/ga/recs/49/53>(last visited Sep. 21, 1998), U.N. GAOR, 84th Plenary Meeting, U.N. Doc. A/RES/49/53 (1994). *See also Resolution Adopted by the General Assembly at* gopher://gopher.un.org/00/ga/recs/51/RES51-EN.207 (last visited Sep. 21, 1998), U.N. GAOR, 51st Sess., Agenda Item 47, U.N. Doc. A/Res/51/207 (1997).

[5] *Report of the Preparatory Committee on the Establishment of an International Criminal Court*, U.N. ICC, Rome, 1998, U.N. Doc. A/Conf.183/2/Add. 1.

[6] *Ibid*, Art. 5, "War Crimes," at 14; Art. 5, "Crimes Against Humanity," at 25.

[7] NGO Family Voice Report, *The United Nations Diplomatic Conference of Plenipotentiaries on the Establishment of an International Criminal Court*, Appendix D, "The Draft ICC Statute: Issues of Concern," & 1, at 1. (The "enforced pregnancy" and "persecution" crimes were not the only troublesome prohibitions in the draft ICC. The draft statute also listed "deprivation of liberty" (a legal concept capable of almost limitless expansion) as a "crime against humanity." This provision alone could have ceded vast policy-making powers to the ICC. Every conceivable governmental regulation (such as restricted access to drugs, pornography, and social welfare benefits) could be characterized by the new international court as some form of official "persecution" or, more likely, as unwarranted "deprivations of liberty.")

[8] The Universal Declaration of Human Rights states that "[m]otherhood and childhood are entitled to special care and assistance." Yet, in recent years when

nations have attempted to follow this long accepted admonition, they are criticized by the U.N. committee that monitors compliance with the Convention on the Elimination of Discrimination Against Women (CEDAW). For example, in this year's session, the CEDAW Committee responded to Croatia's report about its laws designed to provide "special protection for the family and in particular for women in their role as mothers and caregivers," CEDAW/C/1998/I/L. 1/Add. 3 ¶ 7, as follows: "The Committee was particularly concerned about the consistent emphasis placed on women's roles as mothers and caregivers in Croatian legislation pertaining to a variety of areas. While legislative provisions protecting maternity are important, the Committee was concerned that prioritizing that aspect of women's lives reinforced traditional and stereotypical role expectations, which tended to limit women's full participation in society. The Committee commented that despite the fact that women in Croatia were well-educated and participated in the labour force in large numbers, a careful and gender-sensitive analysis of the emphasis on motherhood vis-a-vis women's roles in the public sphere was needed on the part of the Government to assure de facto gender equality in the Croatian society of the future." *Ibid.* at ¶ 25. *See also* A/51/38 ¶ 283 ("While acknowledging the good intentions behind [Ukraine's] legal measures adopted to protect maternity, the Committee was of the view that such measures could be overprotective and detrimental to the status of women in a market-oriented economy.")

[9] For example, one of the authors attended a workshop on gender issues at the most recent session of the Commission on Human Rights in Geneva. The workshop mentioned marriage only in the context of "marital rape."

[10] The CEDAW Committee routinely criticizes countries for placing legal restrictions on abortion, even though CEDAW never mentions abortion as a right. *See, e.g.,* A/51/38 ¶¶ 55 (Cyprus), 131 (Paraguay). In its response to Croatia's report, the CEDAW Committee even implied that a woman's unrecognized right to abortion trumps a physician's right to refuse to perform abortions on religious grounds, stating, "[The Committee] was ... concerned about information regarding the refusal, by some [Croatian] hospitals, to provide abortions on the basis of conscientious objection of doctors. The Committee considered this to be an infringement of women's reproductive rights."

In a recent Round Table report, approved by the heads of all U.N. human rights enforcement bodies, a wholesale reinterpretation of basic human rights documents was proposed. The Round Table Report recommends that the "right to life," the "right to equality before the courts," the "right to freedom of movement," and the "right to protection of privacy and the home" all be interpreted to include a right to abortion. *Round Table of Human Rights Treaty Bodies on Human Rights Approaches to Women's Health, with a Focus on Sexual and Reproductive Health and Rights,* Summary of Proceedings and Recommendations, pp. 22-23.

[11] Despite recent studies showing the declining populations in the developed world, and the resulting economic hardship, reduction of the birth rate is a primary

goal of the U.N. agencies. *See,* e.g., *The State of World Population,* 1998, UNFPA at 20 ("Shrinking Populations' Scare Is Premature").

[12] In the Third World Youth Forum, and at the Conference of Ministers Responsible for Youth (held in Portugal in August 1998), documents were approved calling for "services" and "information dissemination" regarding "reproductive health," including "access to safe, effective, affordable and acceptable legal methods of family planning of their choice." WCMRY/1998/L. 10 ¶ 73. The U.N. agencies guiding these conferences confirmed that they intended to provide the "information" and "services" to children as young as 10. *See* "Youth Health and Development," discussion paper prepared by WHO, UNICEF, UNFPA, UNAIDS, at p. 2, note a. Yet, there was steadfast resistance to any mention of the rights of parents with respect to the education and moral upbringing of their children. *See* Universal Declaration of Human Rights, Art. 26 ¶ 3 ("Parents have a prior right to choose the kind of education that shall be given to their children."); International Covenant on Economic Social and Cultural Rights, Art. 13 ¶ 3 (states to ensure "respect for the liberty of parents ... to ensure the religious and moral education of their children in conformity with their own convictions.").

The report of the *Round Table of Human Rights Treaty Bodies* (*supra* note 10) suggests that language calling for the "protection of children" be interpreted to "ensure adolescent access to sex education and decision-making in respect to reproductive and sexual health services."

The Committee on the Rights of the Child found the United Kingdom out of compliance with the Convention on the Rights of the Child because parents in England and Wales may decide to withdraw their children from public school sex education programs. CRC/C/15/Add. 34.

[13] During the various U.N. meetings touching on social issues, nations from the European Union, and sometimes the United States, routinely attempt to introduce pro-homosexual language. Thus far, such efforts have, for the most part, been thwarted by the Muslim nations.

However, the United Nations human rights organizations have embarked on a concerted effort to reinterpret already accepted human rights documents to include new rights for homosexuals. Mary Robinson, High Commissioner for Human Rights, gave an address on the Universal Declaration of Human Rights, in which she declared that the Declaration addresses "discrimination on grounds of gender or on the basis of sexual orientation." Address at United Nations University, Tokyo, January 27, 1998.

In 1994, in *Toonen v. Tasmania,* CCPR/C/50/D/488/1992, the Human Rights Committee held that the International Covenant on Civil and Political Rights protects the right to homosexual sodomy. This decision was applauded by the heads of the other human rights treaty bodies in the report of the *Round Table of Human Rights Treaty Bodies on Human Rights Approaches to Women's Health, with a Focus on Sexual and Reproductive Health and Rights,* at page 23. In an

NGO Forum held in September 1998, Elizabeth Evatt, a member of the Human Rights Committee, stated that "intolerance of homosexuality was a clear case of discrimination and inequality. It fell clearly within the scope of human rights protection and there should be no debate or controversy." Press Release, NGO/301, PI/1080, September 14, 1998.

[14] The coalition included representatives of international right-to-life groups, as well as family advocacy organizations from the United States, Canada, Great Britain, Europe and South America.

[15] Rhonda Copelon, *Losing the Negative Right of Privacy: Building Sexual and Reproductive Health*, 18 N.Y.U. Rev. L. & Soc. Change 15, 40, 49 (1991).

[16] As originally drafted, Article 5 of the ICC criminalized "persecution" on grounds of "gender," and Article 20, in turn, forbade any "adverse distinction" on the basis of "gender" or "similar grounds." These legal requirements, if unmodified, could have been used to create presently unrecognized, international "gender-based" rights, including international same-sex "marriage" and global invalidation of all laws regulating homosexual behavior.

[17] *Gender*, in western academe, is capable of expansion well beyond traditional conceptions of male and female. Delegates to the Beijing Conference for Women, for example, spent considerable time and effort discussing the precise meaning of *gender*. One of the notions discussed was a conceptual scheme advanced in the work of Anne Fausto-Sterling. She envisioned a new social order where "the sexes have multiplied beyond currently imaginable limits," a world where the classifications of "parent and child, male and female, heterosexual and homosexual" would "have to be dissolved as sources of division" because society "would permit ambiguity in a culture that had overcome sexual division." Anne Fausto-Sterling, *The Five Sexes: Why Male and Female Are Not Enough. Sciences*, Mar.-Apr. 1993, at 20, 24.

[18] *Rome Statute of the International Criminal Court*, Art. 7 & 2(f), at 6.

[19] *Ibid.*, Art. 7 & 3, at 6.

[20] The ICC does not define *gender* simply as "male" and "female," but rather as "male" and "female" in the "context of society." Although the precise meaning of this phrase is presently unknowable, it does provide room to argue that "gender" is not limited exclusively to biology. That means that the ICC definition may once again become open-textured enough to accommodate Fausto-Sterling's "five sexes." *See* discussion at note 17, above.

[21] Copelon, *supra,* note 15, at 49.

[22] *Rome Statute of the International Criminal Court*, Art. 7 & 3, at 6.

[23] *See*, e.g., *Report on the World Social Condition 1997*, U.N. Commission for Social Development, at 156, U.N. Doc. E/95/15.

[24] "Canadians Float Compromise," *Terra Viva*, July 7, 1998, at 1.

[25] *Bowers v. Hardwick*, 478 U.S. 186, 197 (1986) (Burger, C.J., concurring).

[26] United Nations Division for the Advancement of Women, United Nations

Population Fund, United Nations High Commissioner for Human Rights, *Round Table of Human Rights Treaty Bodies on Human Rights Approaches to Women's Health, with a Focus on Sexual and Reproductive Health and Rights* (December 1996) at 22-23. *Accord, id.* at 7, 11, 12, 18, 23-24, 27, 28, 33-34, 36-37. *See also* Symposium on Human Rights in the Asia-Pacific Region, "The Universal Declaration of Human Rights: A Living Document," statement by Mrs. Mary Robinson, United Nations High Commissioner for Human Rights, United Nations University, Tokyo, January 27, 1998. (Although "today's world is more complex than it was fifty years ago," the "agenda set by the [Universal] Declaration [of Human Rights] is surprisingly apt for these new complexities—whether they are linked to the rights of indigenous peoples or the right to development or discrimination on grounds of gender or on the basis of sexual orientation—but who could have imagined in 1948 that we would use the fiftieth anniversary of the Declaration as an opportunity to reposition these fresh concerns and others in our order of priorities?")

Chapter 13

Human Rights and the Gender Perspective

Dale O'Leary

This year, we celebrate the fiftieth anniversary of the United Nations' Universal Declaration of Human Rights. This document sets a universal standard by which to judge behavior. It also fosters respect for the *concept* of human rights, although we are far from a world that uniformly observes them.

Women are among the principal beneficiaries of the increased respect for human rights. Today, only a very few countries deny women the right to vote, the right to pursue education, or the right to work outside the home in a profession of choice. The cause of women's rights, however, and all the goodwill associated with it, is now being exploited by radical feminists, whose interests do not include the true well-being of women. Instead, radical feminists focus on a "gender agenda" which violates the Declaration's vision for women, family, and human dignity.

This gender agenda is primarily about pretending there are no differences between men and women, and destroying the family as we

Dale O'Leary is a freelance writer, lecturer, and author of The Gender Agenda: Redefining Equality, *which contains her analysis of the feminist agenda and her experiences at the U.N. conferences in Cairo and Beijing.*

know it. Radical feminists want to re-interpret the Universal Declaration of Human Rights to include this agenda and thereby force it upon people around the world. Indeed, Mary Robinson, the new High Commissioner for Human Rights and the former President of Ireland, has suggested that certain "values," including the "complexities" of "gender" and "sexual orientation," are *implied* in the Universal Declaration.[1] There is no need, therefore, to make a new declaration to recognize these values: *Reinterpretation* of the original will suffice. Thus it is that the Declaration has become a political tool for those in power at the U.N., rather than a statement of ideals to be shared by all the world.

This essay is an attempt to explain how this state of affairs came to pass and how those of us who care about motherhood and the family can do something about it.

HUMAN RIGHTS AS POLITICAL WEAPONS

At the outset, however, we must realize that the words of the Universal Declaration only have power because they represent a reality that transcends governments, political factions, and ideologies. "There is a tendency to believe that society itself has formulated what is known as human rights," Archbishop Martino, Permanent Observer of the Holy See to the United Nations, has warned. In fact, human rights are not a human creation. They are "inherent to the dignity of the human person."[2]

It is not surprising that power-hungry groups use the powerful concept of human rights and the Universal Declaration to hide less laudable ideological goals. Once words are hijacked in this way, however, they can no longer represent a "universal." They become mere political weapons.

That is the big story at the United Nations today. Countless documents and resolutions, including the Universal Declaration, have become political tools. They are being reinterpreted to become products of unbending, radical ideologies that are increasingly divorced from reality and divorced from the beliefs of ordinary people.

For example, radical feminists and their allies now claim that respect for human rights, and for the concept of equality in particular, requires the "mainstreaming of the gender perspective" into all policies and programs.[3] What exactly is this "gender perspective"? Will it secure women's equal human rights or will it undermine women's freedom?

To answer these questions, one needs to understand some history of the "gender perspective" and of those who now promote it.

THE WOMEN'S MOVEMENT AND RADICAL FEMINISM

In the 1960s, a rejuvenated women's movement fought for equal rights, equal opportunity, equal pay for equal work, and equal protection under the law. In the 1970s, however, this movement was taken over by radicals who believe that class differences are the cause of all evil. According to this radical feminist perspective, if a group is divided into different classes, one of these classes will feel inferior. Feeling inferior is oppressive and should be eliminated.

If men and women are different, for example, because women bear children and take care of them, then women are oppressed. The only way to eliminate women's oppression, then, is to eliminate motherhood as women's work. According to this theory, two things are necessary: (1) all women must work at paid labor, and (2) men must assume 50 percent of the direct childcare tasks within the home.[4]

From their beginnings, radical feminists recognized that ordinary women would reject this agenda. When asked whether feminists should support the choice of women to stay at home as full-time mothers, Simone de Beauvoir replied: "[W]e don't believe that any woman should have this choice. No woman should be authorized to stay at home to raise her children. Society should be totally different. Women should not have that choice, precisely because if there is such a choice, too many women will make that one."[5]

Radical feminists explain away the resistance of ordinary women by insisting that women who want to be full-time mothers are brainwashed by a social system created by men. Alison Jagger, author of a textbook on feminism, believes that women's "desires and interests are socially constituted" and most women are "systematically self-deceived" about "truth, morality or even their own interests."[6] According to Jagger, only the radical feminists are not deceived since they have transcended the "theoretical constructs of male dominance."[7]

Simply put, radical feminists believe that women who want to marry and have children have been deluded and deceived by men and do not know what is good for them. Women who do not want these things are free from such delusion. These free women intend to liberate their duped, counterpart sisters from their desires for family and motherhood, whether they like it or not.

This attitude reflects, of course, a disregard for human rights that is typical of the far left. Radicals concern themselves with perceived oppressed classes, not the rights and dignities of individuals. They do not care about or respect individual liberty, human dignity, or even the inalienable right to life. All these rights belong to each human person, not an abstract class. Indeed, as the above indicates, radical feminists are ready to sacrifice human rights in the name of rescuing the group. In this way, they pose a real threat to authentic human rights.

THE RADICAL FEMINIST STRATEGY

Because this revolutionary ideology failed to win popular acceptance, radical feminists began to target institutions relatively immune to public opinion, such as universities, entrenched bureaucracies, and the United Nations. Thus began the long march through the institutions.

At the United Nations, they faced little opposition. Bureaucrats who run daily operations there are highly sympathetic to feminist goals. In fact, many U.N. staffers participate in radical feminist groups and activities.[8] These bureaucrats are not responsive to voters, and national delegations have little control over them. Needless to say, radical feminist NGOs have been able to lobby for their agenda very successfully at U.N. headquarters in New York and at various U.N. conferences around the world.

THE GENDER PERSPECTIVE: THE ABOLITION OF MOTHERHOOD

Radical feminists claim to represent the interests of all women and are thereby able to exploit the general goodwill toward women's rights. Publicly, they blur the differences between their ideological goals and the aspirations of ordinary women. Rather than state their goals openly, they use the phrase "the gender perspective" to hide them.

One can find the United Nations' definition of the "gender perspective," however, in a booklet entitled *Gender Concepts in Development Planning: Basic Approach* (hereafter *Gender Concepts*).[9] According to the booklet,

> [T]o adopt a gender perspective is to distinguish between what is natural and biological and what is socially and culturally constructed, and in the process to re-negotiate the boundaries between the natural (hence relatively inflexible) and the social (and hence relatively transformable).[10]

At first blush, this doesn't sound particularly threatening. Most people believe, for example, that women should not be barred from professional work (what is "culturally constructed") simply because they are women (a natural condition).

It becomes clear, however, that the intention of the authors is actually to ignore the differences between men and women and to transform traditional motherhood.

Shulamith Firestone, one of the founders of the radical feminist movement, is matter-of-fact about the true radical feminist goal: It is a future where "genital differences between human beings no longer matter culturally."[11] This means, of course, opposing any suggestion that men and women are different. With respect to traditional motherhood, the text includes the following: "Nothing in the fact that women bear children implies that they should care for them throughout childhood."[12]

The writers of *Gender Concepts* attempt to impose this mentality by promoting programs that emphasize "strategic gender interests" instead of the focus of the "majority of development initiatives directed at women, [which] are primarily intended to satisfy practical needs."[13] Women's practical needs include such things as housing, food for families, and access to clean water. Women's strategic gender interests include such things as abolition of the "sexual division of labor" and "freedom of reproductive choice."[14] The sexual division of labor refers to the family where the father and mother divide the work of the family and the mother accepts primary responsibility for the care of children. The abolition of this sexual division of labor amounts to the abolition of motherhood.

THE GENDER PERSPECTIVE: A RADICAL DEPARTURE FROM THE UNIVERSAL DECLARATION OF HUMAN RIGHTS

The authors of *Gender Concepts* never quite say this. They begin their booklet with an appeal to the accepted and respected concepts of equal rights and human rights. There is a critical difference, however, between human rights as understood by most people and as understood by the authors of *Gender Concepts*.

For example, Article 16 of the Universal Declaration of Human Rights reads, in part, "Men and women ... have a right to marry and to found a family."[15] Obviously, the authors of the Declaration believed men and women were different and distinct, since they refer to men *and* women. They also clearly believed that genital differences mattered, since without them and their corresponding differences, there would be no founding of families. These are fundamental and legitimate assumptions. The drafters of *Gender Concepts*, however, reject and challenge them. Their goals are simply at odds with the human rights vision of the Declaration.

Similarly, Article 25 states, "Motherhood and childhood are entitled to special care and assistance."[16] This Article reveals a basic belief that motherhood is inherently different from fatherhood. The drafters could have written, "Fatherhood is entitled to special care and assistance." They did not. They asserted, instead, that mothers are somehow special and should receive special care and special protection from society.

Few realize how far radical feminists are taking us from the ideals expressed in the Universal Declaration. The radicals benefit enormously from this ignorance. Their goals, if public and open, would undoubtedly meet resistance. But they are in command of many of the procedures and agendas at U.N. conferences and conventions. In this way, they are able to enact their program, item by item.

For example, radical feminists controlled the United Nations' Beijing Conference for Women. The resulting Platform for Action called for "mainstreaming the gender perspective" and promoted the radical feminist ideology. Paragraph 28 states: "In many countries, the differences between women's and men's achievements and activities are still not recognized as the consequence of socially constructed gender roles rather than immutable biological differences." [17] This is the radical feminist way of attacking motherhood as a unique vocation of women. *Socially constructed gender roles* means *motherhood*, which the Platform describes in the most demeaning of terms. Few delegates, in voting for such language, realize they are committing themselves and their nations to this attack. But that is precisely what is at the heart of "mainstreaming the gender perspective."

It should be noted, too, that an attack on motherhood as the particular work of women is an attack on marriage and family as we know it. It is not surprising that this same Platform document has hundreds of references to *gender*, but not one word of support for women who care for their own children as their primary work. By supporting all family arrangements but this one, the document in effect undermines the traditional family. This, of course, is the intention of the radical feminists. One simply cannot ignore the perversity of a document which supposedly reflects the concerns of the world's women, but where the words *wife* and *husband* never appear.

OPPOSING THE GENDER PERSPECTIVE

In many parts of the world, women are just beginning to experience the benefits of the new respect for human rights. If radical feminists in the United Nations continue their efforts to impose the "gender perspective" as part of human rights, they will not succeed, as they hope, in destroying women's desires to care for their own children. Instead, they will destroy respect for real human rights. And women will be the victims.

As Archbishop Martino has suggested, human rights are not a human construct: They are natural rights that precede and transcend politics. The radical feminist pretense that human rights are just political, to be manipulated in service of ideological goals, will inevitably displace efforts to further observance of real human rights. The most devastating harm will be to people, especially women, for whom respect is just beginning to develop as a matter of human rights. We cannot let that happen.

The challenge for family advocates is to inform ordinary people about how dangerous the "gender perspective" really is, on the one hand, and about how important real human rights are, on the other. Defenders of the family must make it clear that *we* are the defenders of real human rights. We understand, too, that, when human rights are manipulated for political purposes, real human rights and real people suffer.

Finally, we need to make it clear that, when we fight for motherhood, for marriage, and for the family, we are fighting for women.

ENDNOTES

[1] Mary Robinson, speech, Symposium on Human Rights in the Asia Pacific, University of Tokyo, 27 Jan. 1998 (emphasis added).

[2] Archbishop Renato R. Martino, statement, 49th Session of the General Assembly of the United Nations, 30 Nov. 1994.

[3] On December 12, 1997, the U.N. General Assembly adopted a resolution calling for the "mainstreaming of the gender perspective" in order "to create a peaceful, just and humane world based on all human rights and fundamental

freedoms, including the principle of equality." United Nations, General Assembly Resolution 52/100, 12 Dec. 1997.

[4] Shulamith Firestone, *The Dialectic of Sex* (New York: Bantam Books, 1970). *See also* Nancy Chodorow, *The Reproduction of Mothering* (Berkeley: University of California Press, 1978) and Susan Okin, "Change the Family, Change the World," *Utne Reader* March/April 1990.

[5] Christina Hoff Sommers, *Who Stole Feminism?* (New York: Simon & Schuster 1994) 256.

[6] Alison Jagger, "Political Philosophies of Women's Liberation," *Feminism and Philosophy* (Totowa, NJ: Littlefield, Adams & Co. 1977) 14.

[7] *Id.*

[8] In December 1994, for example, the feminist lobbying groups held a strategy meeting in Glenn Cove, New York. They posted the list of attendees on the Internet. Ten percent of those participating were U.N. employees.

[9] INSTRAW (The United Nations International Research and Training Institute for the Advancement of Women), *Gender Concepts in Development Planning: Basic Approach,* July 1995.

[10] *Id.* at 11 (quoting Naila Kabeer, paper, "Gender, Development and Training: Raising Awareness in Development Planning," The National Labour Institute/Ford Foundation Workshop of Gender Training and Development (Bangalore Nov. 29 - Dec. 6 1990). Found in GADU, Newspack No. 14 Oxfam, Oxford.

[11] Firestone, *supra* note 4.

[12] *Supra* note 9 (quoting Maureen Mackintosh, "Gender and Economics: The Sexual Division of Labour and the Subordination of Women," in *Of Marriage and the Market,* Eds. Young, *et al.* (London: 1981), 181.

[13] *Supra* note 9.

[14] *Id.*

[15] United Nations, *Universal Declaration of Human Rights*, 1948.

[16] *Id.*

[17] United Nations, *Fourth World Conference on Women*, Sept. 1995.

Chapter 14

Homosexuality Is *Not* A "Universal Human Right"

Tom McFeely

In a speech delivered August 28 at a Geneva conference commemorating the fiftieth anniversary of the Universal Declaration of Human Rights (UDHR), United Nations High Commissioner of Human Rights Mary Robinson commented, "It is precisely this notion of 'universality'—in the widest sense—that gives [the UDHR] its force." Ms. Robinson also accurately noted that the UDHR had been deliberately crafted by its drafters as "a distillation of many of the values inherent in the world's major legal systems and religious beliefs, including the Buddhist, Christian, Hindu, Islamic and Jewish traditions."[1]

Her remarks ring more than a little ironic, given that Ms. Robinson herself is one of the most prominent members of the cadre of key U.N. officials who are lobbying vigorously for the inclusion of homosexuality as part of the corpus of universal, internationally recognized human rights.[2] After all, whatever else might be said about the current campaign

Tom McFeely is a Canadian journalist and researcher with extensive experience in monitoring U.N. affairs. He is a member of the Parliamentary Press Gallery of Canada and is senior editor for the Report News Magazine.

by homosexual activists and their allies to legitimize homosexual activity, there can be little doubt that it fails the test of universality cited by the High Commissioner. Indeed, the "gay rights" agenda comprehensively transgresses against the "inherent values" of many of the world's legal systems, and against the beliefs of at least three of the great world religions that she named.

How is it, then, that key U.N. officials like Ms. Robinson can so casually advance an agenda that so obviously contradicts their own definition of what constitutes a universal human right? And what damage is being caused, both to the health of human societies and to the proper understanding of legitimate human rights, as a result of the United Nations' advancement of the fraudulent "right" to engage in homosexual activity without legal or social sanctions?

A CAMPAIGN OF STEALTH

Necessarily, much of the U.N. effort to advance homosexual "rights" has been covert in nature. This is because a large proportion of the world's nations, particularly those that are predominantly Catholic and Muslim, still regard homosexual behavior as entirely aberrant and have no intention of legitimizing it.

DEFINITIONAL SUBTERFUGE: "ORIENTATION," "GENDER," AND "VARIOUS FORMS OF THE FAMILY"

U.N. proponents of so-called "gay rights" consequently employ a variety of definitional subterfuges. The first is the term *sexual orientation*, which has begun to be used in many Western jurisdictions as a prohibited ground of discrimination under human rights legislation.[3] But this term is deliberately confusing and inaccurate, as what is really under debate is not discrimination against sexual "orientation"— something that is impossible to establish unless an individual chooses to publicize his sexual proclivities—but rather discrimination against homosexual *behavior*.

Still, the substitution of *orientation* for *behavior* has obvious advantages from the perspective of homosexual rights lobbyists. First, it allows homosexuality to be more easily added to the list of proscribed characteristics for discrimination, which predominantly consist of immutable characteristics like race and sex, and abstract concepts like political and religious beliefs, rather than specific behaviors. It also buttresses the scientifically flimsy claim of activists that the predilection towards homosexual activity is a consequence of a genetically predetermined "orientation" over which the individual involved has no control.

But since the "orientation" camouflage often remains inadequate in terms of persuading religiously based nations to drop their objections to the advancement of homosexuality, even more vague and confusing terms regularly intrude into U.N. discussions. For example, Western delegations to recent U.N. conferences have striven to replace references to *family* with alternatives like *various forms of the family*. They have also striven to include *gender* references whenever possible in contexts that might pertain to homosexual issues. *Various forms of the family* is intended to legitimize homosexual "marriage" as a valid variant of "family," while *gender* is defined by pro-homosexual activists within the U.N. system as including homosexuals, bisexuals and the "transgendered," as well as the traditional sexes of male and female.[4]

Along with the definitional confusion sown by pro-homosexual lobbyists, the support of the powerful radical feminist contingent within the United Nations has been integral to the growing acceptance of homosexual "rights" at the international level. In part, this is because many leading feminist ideologues are themselves lesbians, and acceptance of female homosexuality has consequently been a central radical feminist demand for decades.[5] Moreover, homosexual conduct has the key benefit, both from the point of view of radical feminists and that of population control advocates, who constitute another dominant U.N. lobby, that it normally does not result in any progeny who might "enslave" their mothers or make new demands on the world's allegedly overtaxed resource base.

A "REINTERPRETATION" OF THE UNIVERSAL DECLARATION

In her series of recent speeches marking the fiftieth anniversary of the UDHR, Mary Robinson has demonstrated the strategy that U.N. agencies have adopted in promoting homosexual "rights." Rather than strive openly for a comprehensive new document that would explicitly recognize "sexual orientation" and other contentious elements of the human rights agenda being advanced by social liberals, the intent is to seek redefinitions of the UDHR and other key international human rights documents.[6] Laudable though the UDHR may have been, the activists argue, it was really only the starting point for the delineation of the corpus of universal human rights, which they allege has expanded greatly since 1948. Thus the desire of pro-homosexuality advocates to "seed" every new U.N. document with as much supportive *various forms of the family* and *gender* terminology as possible, so that this terminology can be cited as "evidence" that the world community has already acknowledged concepts like "sexual orientation" and homosexual "marriage."

Homosexual activists have already achieved considerable success at the national level by operating in a similar fashion. Because the attainment of their goals through free and informed political debates has often proved impossible, even in countries as sympathetic as Canada, lobbyists frequently have relied instead on the reading of homosexual "rights" into existing legislation by sympathetic courts and human rights tribunals. A striking example of the success of this approach occurred this spring, when the Supreme Court of Canada ruled that the human rights statute of the province of Alberta must be amended to protect "sexual orientation" —even though the government that passed the legislation and the current provincial government both explicitly opposed such recognition.[7] Indeed, one of the chief reasons homosexual lobbyists attach so much importance to winning recognition at the U.N. level is to strengthen their hand when arguing these kinds of precedent-setting cases before politically unaccountable tribunals.

HOMOSEXUAL RIGHTS HAVE A HIGH COST

Along with the most obvious negative consequence of the legitimization of homosexual conduct—the physical and psychological injuries that are documented corollaries of such behaviors, through calamities such as the AIDS epidemic now raging among male homosexuals—the advancement of the homosexual "rights" campaign is exacting other penalties.

UNDERMINING THE AUTHENTIC BODY OF HUMAN RIGHTS

For one thing, to claim "universality" for a "right" that does not enjoy majority support even in many Western countries, and that has virtually no backing whatsoever in scores of more traditionally minded nations, clearly devalues the entire notion of a body of universal human rights. And the continued persistence of Western liberals in passing off their parochial agendas as being of universal application—and the exploitation of U.N. agencies such as Ms. Robinson's Office of the High Commissioner of Human Rights to foist these agendas on other countries—risks undermining all of the advances that have been made in the postwar period in encouraging the world's nations to respect those human rights that really are transcendent in character.

CONFLICT WITH RELIGIOUS FREEDOM

But the injuries to the proper understanding of human rights scarcely stop there. Recognition of homosexuality as a universal right must necessarily conflict with the right to religious freedom, guaranteed in Article 18 of the UDHR. As noted earlier, orthodox Christianity, Judaism and Islam all explicitly condemn homosexual behavior. Moreover, homosexual activists themselves harbor no illusions about the fact that these rights must necessarily collide. According to an article published in December 1997 in the Canadian homosexual newspaper *Xtra West*, lesbian lawyer Barbara Findlay predicted bluntly that "the legal struggle for queer rights will one day be a showdown between freedom of religion versus sexual orientation."[8]

THE TRADITIONAL FAMILY, PARENTAL AUTHORITY AND EDUCATION

Other elements of the UDHR will also come under implicit assault, such as the recognition afforded to "the family" as "the natural and fundamental unit of society" in Article 16.3. Any bid by a given country to retain the traditional understanding of the family as being based on the heterosexual couple will be held to constitute improper "discrimination," once homosexuality wins full human rights recognition. This is so despite the fact that no serious analysis of the intent of the UDHR's drafters could ever support the contention that they intended to recognize cohabiting homosexuals as constituting a "natural and fundamental" social unit. Also in jeopardy would be the "prior right" of parents to "choose the kind of education that shall be given to their children," as guaranteed under Article 26.3. Parental exercise of that prior right in such a way as to protect children from the proliferation of homosexual propaganda that is now engulfing public school systems throughout western Europe and North America would be held to transgress against the new international prohibitions being advanced by U.N. bodies against "homophobia."[9]

If and when a showdown occurs between traditional concepts of human rights and novel concepts like "sexual orientation," the U.N.'s human rights advocates have already signaled which ones they believe should be accorded precedence. The United Nations' 1996 "Round Table of Human

Rights Treaty Bodies on Human Rights Approaches to Women's Health" asserted on page 7, "A human rights approach to women's health creates an international standard that transcends culture, tradition and social norms. Although these forces may bind societies together, they cannot justify value systems which perpetuate women's subordination."[10] That is to say, "rights" to abortion and homosexual conduct must "transcend" the objections of traditional morality, irrespective of the fact that the vast majority of the members of a given society might subscribe to that traditional morality.

THE DECONSTRUCTION OF THE MEANING OF SEXUALITY—AND OF HUMAN RIGHTS

While the advancement of homosexuality as a legitimate and healthy expression of sexuality can be regarded as perhaps the most egregiously perverse redefinition of *universal human rights,* it must be acknowledged that this redefinition could only occur within the context of a much broader breakdown in the moral understanding of sexuality. Since the 1960s, under the pressure of easy access to the contraceptive Pill and the challenge of radical feminism to the traditional understanding of woman's role as wife and mother, Western societies have sanctioned a variety of policies that have tended to divorce human sexual activity from its traditional procreative function. The unhappy consequences of this "culture of death," as Pope John Paul II has so eloquently characterized it, are manifold, including epidemic rates of abortion, teenage pregnancies, sexually transmitted diseases, and family disintegration.

In fact, it can be argued that the acceptance of homosexual activity was an inevitability in such a context. In the absence of a coherent understanding of sexuality as a faculty intended to unite a married couple, and to enable that couple to cooperate with God in the creation of new human life, every traditional restriction on sexual behavior can logically be expected to be washed away. That such an erosion would necessarily occur was anticipated by the Roman Catholic Church, most notably in the 1968 papal encyclical *Humanae Vitae.*[11]

The effort to legitimize homosexuality has had a particularly corrosive effect on the intellectual understanding of what constitutes a universal human right. This is because homosexual activity, by its very nature, is destructive physically, psychologically and socially. Other universal human rights have properly been embraced by the human community because they are viewed as fundamental to the welfare of individuals and societies. The embrace of homosexuality, in contrast, requires a willful disregard for the welfare of the individuals and societies who engage in its practice. By condoning at the international level this destructive embrace, U.N. agencies are contributing actively to the disintegration of the very meaning of the concept of universal human rights.

ENDNOTES

[1] Mary Robinson, keynote address to "FORUM 98: Fifty Years after the Universal Declaration of Human Rights," Geneva, August 28, 1998.

[2] Ms. Robinson has lobbied for recognition of "sexual orientation" as a protected ground against discrimination on a number of recent occasions, including notably her official remarks to the 54th Session of the U.N. Commission on Human Rights in March 1998. The reinterpretation of human rights documents to include homosexuality was also specifically addressed on p. 18 and p. 23 of the "Round Table of Human Rights Treaty Bodies on Human Rights Approaches to Women's Health, with a Focus on Sexual and Reproductive Health and Rights." The Round Table, which took place in Glen Cove, New York, in December 1996, was sponsored by the U.N. Division for the Advancement of Women, the U.N. Population Fund and the U.N. High Commissioner for Human Rights, and included representatives of all six U.N. treaty bodies charged with monitoring human rights issues.

As well, in a 1994 ruling on the case of *Toonen vs. Australia*, the U.N. Human Rights Committee concluded that the anti-sodomy statute of the state of Tasmania was a violation of Australia's obligations under Articles 2 and 17 of the International Covenant on Civil and Political Rights.

Homosexual "rights" have also been recognized by the U.N. High Commission for Refugees, which declared in its publication "Protecting Refugees," "Homosexuals may be eligible for refugee status on the basis of persecution because of their membership in a particular social group. It is the policy of UNHCR that persons facing attack, inhumane treatment or serious discrimination because of their homosexuality, and whose governments are unable or unwilling to protect them, should be recognized as refugees."

[3] The term has been used in a wide number of U.N. contexts, including those noted in the previous endnote. In 1996, Canada amended the Canadian Human Rights Act to prohibit discrimination based on "sexual orientation" by federally regulated employers, landlords and services. Several Canadian provinces and several U.S. states have enacted similar prohibitions, as have a number of European nations.

[4] A protracted debate occurred during the recent International Criminal Court negotiations, which took place in Rome from June 15 to July 17, 1998, over the inclusion of references to *gender* in a number of articles of the ICC Statute. Predominantly Muslim and Catholic nations insisted that if *gender* was to be

included, it must be defined to mean nothing more than "the two sexes, male and female." Western countries strenuously objected to this effort to circumscribe *gender* to exclude a homosexual meaning. A compromise was eventually struck, with *gender* defined as meaning "the two sexes, male and female, in the context of society."

Similar disputes over efforts to substitute phrases like *various forms of the family* for *the family* have erupted at recent U.N. conferences, such as the 1996 Habitat II conference in Istanbul, where Pope John Paul II's personal spokesman, Dr. Joaquin Navarro-Valls, publicly condemned Canada's refusal to allow a reference to *family* to be incorporated in the final document. As well, some U.N. documents have openly advocated the recognition of homosexual "families." In "Family: Challenges for the Future," a document prepared in 1992 by the U.N.'s International Year of the Family Secretariat, "same-gender" families are formally recognized as a legitimate family form. According to the document, "rather than indicating an erosion of the worth of the family," these "new forms of family life are developing to meet the challenges of the modern world."

[5] For instance, an article titled "Why Reproductive Health and Rights: Because I Am a Woman," by Marge Berer in the November 1997 issue of the feminist journal *Reproductive Health Matters* details her experiences as an activist in Britain in the 1970s as the "women's liberation movement" gained influence there. She recounts that one of the "Seven Demands of the Women's Liberation Movement" formulated during that period was "an end to all discrimination against lesbians."

[6] Both Ms. Robinson, in her recent speeches regarding the UDHR, and the Round Table of Human Rights Treaty Bodies, argued specifically that existing human rights documents can be reinterpreted to accommodate novel "universal human rights" like "sexual orientation."

[7] Joe Woodard, "Ralph gets moral, and Alberta gets gay rights," *Alberta Report*, April 20, 1998, pp. 12-17.

[8] "Final push needed, Findlay says," *Xtra West*, January 8, 1998, p. 8.

[9] One recent example of the United Nations' employment of proscriptions against "homophobia" occurred in the preamble of the Braga Youth Action Plan, which was the document produced by the U.N.-sponsored Third World Conference on Youth, held in Braga, Portugal, August 2-6, 1998. The "homophobia" reference was mysteriously inserted into the final version of the Action Plan, even though the youth delegates in attendance had never debated whether or not it should be incorporated into the document.

[10] "Round Table of Human Rights Treaty Bodies," *op. cit*, p. 7.

[11] Encyclical Letter of Paul VI, *Humanae Vitae,* Article 17, "Grave Consequences of Methods of Artificial Birth Control."

Chapter 15

Population Control Efforts: A Gross Abuse of Human Rights

David Morrison

Whereas disregard and contempt for human rights have resulted in barbarous acts which have outraged the conscience of mankind ...

Thus begins the second paragraph of the Preamble to the United Nations' Universal Declaration of Human Rights, a document whose fiftieth anniversary the United Nations celebrates this year. It feels odd, in the waning days of humanity's bloodiest century, to read the document's list of high ideals and proposed freedoms. The intervening years, even within the United Nations itself, have been filled with so many wrongs.

A person in the wake of a binge often turns strongly, for a while, away from drinking. So too did an idealistic international coalition turn away from the blood-soaked years that immediately preceded

David Morrison is the editor of Population Research Institute Review, *the monthly newsletter of the Population Research Institute, a non-profit educational and research organization dedicated to presenting the truth about population-related issues.*

1948. Less than three years earlier, American cameras recorded for eternity the hollow eyes of Buchenwald's incredulous survivors, and in the blink of an eye, whole Japanese cities had been wiped from the face of the earth. The authors of the Universal Declaration hoped they had seen the last of such carnage.

IDEOLOGY VS. HUMAN RIGHTS

The passing years revealed that the United Nations' comprehension of the Universal Declaration lagged behind its authors' idealism. The spirit of the 1948 signatories was willing enough, but U.N. moral and intellectual commitment to the ideal in time grew weak. Post-Declaration U.N. activities reveal that the organization lacks the crucial understanding to become a voice for individual rights in what remains a savage world.

The recognition of the inherent dignity of human rights, the Declaration proclaims, serves as "the foundation of freedom." Thus, we must never deem human rights, the very foundation of human freedom, as mere adjuncts to some larger agenda—even an agenda enacted in the name of improving humanity's lot—which has been the stated goal of so many totalitarian regimes. Whether by starving kulaks in the Ukraine, rounding up Jews in Warsaw, raping Chinese girls in Nanking, or leaving elderly Japanese to die interned in California, this century has witnessed the use of humanity itself as a pawn for competing ideologies.

In the end, humanity's most important question is not whether fascism or communism, socialism or capitalism, environmentalism, feminism, materialism or multiculturalism will prevail. The most important question is whether our "global village" will recognize the primacy of authentic human rights, which cradle human freedom, over these ideologies. No cause is so good or so necessary that the dignity and inherent rights of human beings should be sacrificed for it.

Unfortunately, the United Nations doesn't feel that way. It has failed to confront the ideological forces that now control it and that have led it to stray far from the Declaration's vision of faith in fundamental human rights. The most dominant of these forces is the population control lobby. This force is utterly consumed by its agenda to curb population growth and believes that all other goals should serve this one. Its dominance at the United Nations means that this ideology, not an authentic human rights vision, guides the United Nations' interpretation of the Universal Declaration. Not surprisingly, human rights abuses occur as a result. Very few in U.N. circles ever question the essential premise of this ideology: that the world contains, or may soon contain, "too many people." This alone is sad evidence that the United Nations and other international institutions have chosen, either passively or actively, to take the side of ideology over human rights.

THE CASE OF CHINA

Consider for a moment just the case of the United Nations and China. China is one of more than 30 nations that sacrifices human rights on the altar of alleged overpopulation. Its so-called "family planning" program is the most comprehensive, the largest, and arguably the most egregious. Two generations of Chinese men and women have been forced into abortion or sterilization with threats of fines, imprisonment, loss of home, or even loss of life.

To these Chinese, Article 16 of the Universal Declaration, which proclaims that "men and women have a right to marry and to found a family," is just so many words. To Chi An, a 38-year-old Chinese mother living temporarily in the United States, who received a letter from her "family planning office" demanding that she abort her second child, the Declaration is a tragic, unfulfilled promise.

It would be unjust, of course, to lay the responsibility for China's population control brutality at the United Nations' door if, for example, the U.N. Secretary General or even the United Nations Population Fund (UNFPA, the United Nations' population control arm) had worked to overturn the policy, or had, at the very least, denounced it. But they have not.

Indeed, not only has the United Nations remained silent, but it has even cooperated with the policy. For example, UNFPA and the Chinese government published the booklet *Training Family Planning Counselors in China*, jointly with China's State Family Planning Commission and the Program for Appropriate Technology in Health (PATH), which is funded by the U.S. Government. (The United States has contracted approximately $34 million in agreements dating from 1990 to 1999, according to the U.S. Agency for International Development's Office of Procurement.) The authors, all of whom belong to UNFPA, the Chinese government, or PATH, glowingly describe a program of "training the trainers" of rural "family planning programs." According to this booklet, developing the "interpersonal communication and counseling" skills of family planning workers is critical. It encourages counselors to lull Chinese women into compliance with the government's severe one-child policy. This, presumably, is a more effective mode of enforcement than the bullying, intimidation and threats that have been the enforcement method of choice in years gone by.

The UNFPA does not stop there. In early 1998, it announced that it would spend $20 million on an "experiment" in which the ever-controlling Chinese government would no longer force mothers in 32 counties to ask permission to give birth. The UNFPA billed this as a great improvement. "The government of China is keen to move away from its administrative approach to family planning, to an integrated, client centered approach," said Kerstin Trone, a UNFPA program director.

Make no mistake: The Chinese population control policy and goals remain unchanged. That the strategy of the government has changed is almost insignificant. Other pressures favoring abortion and sterilization, more subtle and sometimes more insidious, remain. For example, the Chinese government continues to deny necessary papers, including identity cards, to so-called "illegal" children. It limits the job opportunities of those not submitting to the plan. And it prohibits, by law, the adoption of "illegal" children, except by foreigners who pay the requisite fees. The UNFPA, by its silence, implicitly endorses these pressures and goals.

This is unacceptable. The United Nations has the right (indeed, the responsibility) to speak out against a government that tramples human rights in this way. When will the women of Tibet benefit from the protections of the Declaration if the UNFPA continues its present course?[1]

STERILIZATION CAMPAIGNS: MORE DEAFENING SILENCE

It is, of course, not just the women of China who suffer from the policies of the population control lobby.

In Peru, a huge coercive sterilization campaign has put tens of thousands of Peruvian women at risk for fatal infection. Reports are that 18 are known to have died.[2] The *modus operandi* of this campaign has remained the same in dozens of small villages and poor neighborhoods across the country: The Ministry of Health targets the homes of the poor, or of women who have more than two or three children. Officials begin to visit these homes, again and again, to demand that the women submit to sterilization.[3] They sometimes offer poor women food, clothing, and other supplies in exchange for undergoing the operation.[4] In one case, a mother reported that her child had been enrolled in a nutrition program, only to be expelled when she refused sterilization.

This sterilization campaign only recently "collapsed," accordingly to government reports.[5] Thousands of women have been its victims.

But surely, U.N. defenders will say, the United Nations is not responsible for this program. They should talk to the family of Juana Chero, a mother who lived in the tiny Peruvian hamlet of La Quinta. She resisted the pressure for sterilization for months, but finally succumbed in July 1997. She was taken to a building that bore a prominent plaque: "Project of the UNFPA." She underwent the unsanitary and painful surgery, only to die from complications later that night. Still, UNFPA offered no comment about the atrocities taking place in its building. There can be no question that the UNFPA creates an infrastructure and fosters an attitude that allows, even encourages, such sterilization campaigns to occur.

Cases abound in other parts of the world as well. Where was the United Nations when women were coerced or bribed in Kerala, India, into sterilizations carried out under conditions not fit for animals?[6] Women report that they had to move themselves from one operating table to another and then lay on filthy floors with sheets during the "post-operative" period. Each surgery took an average of two minutes and 40 seconds to complete.[7]

The United Nations has also said nothing about the population control programs in Haiti and Bangladesh. The British Broadcasting Corporation documented the plight of women there who were lied to about Norplant as part of an alleged research project.[8] So-called health officials inserted Norplant in the arms of women without providing any information about the experimental nature of the project or the potential for complications. Countless women became sick from the insertions, some even near death. Officials still refused to remove them. Reports based on this "research" later concluded, "Norplant is a contraceptive method well suited" to Haitian and Bangladeshi women.[9]

Similarly, no word of protest came when the U.S. Agency for International Development (USAID) arranged for the discount purchase and shipment of 70,000 unsterilized and thus potentially lethal intrauterine devices (Dalkon Shields) into the developing world in the 1970s.

One would think that the health arm of the United Nations, the World Health Organization (WHO), if not UNFPA, or USAID, or *someone* at the United Nations, would at least voice some concern about these practices and the resulting human rights abuses. But nothing is heard.

THE ROLE OF THE UNITED NATIONS AND THE PROMISE OF THE UNIVERSAL DECLARATION

These women—in Peru, in India, in Bangladesh, in Haiti, and in other developing countries—are among the poorest and weakest in our world. They can take nothing for granted. Their rights are easy to ignore. The Universal Declaration exists for them. The United Nations has the duty to defend them in particular, for they have no other voice.

The above describes only a few instances of a much larger international pattern that has been in place for more than 30 years. Any so-called "family planning" program in the world today that is not coercive must be considered a nearly complete aberration.

What exactly should we say of the United Nations' role in all this?

In the last 30 years, an enormous superstructure has been built to support the myths of the population control lobby. Governments, foundations, universities, the United Nations, and much of the international media now have an interest in reasserting the alleged and specious link between lower birth rates and economic prosperity. This, at times, pits population control entities against those who hold a more objective view within the United Nations. The UNFPA, for example, often asserts expected levels of population growth that are at odds with the projections published by the United Nations Population Division. Interestingly, at a recent meeting of international demographers in New York, the discussion concerned not the problems of too many people, but the problems of too few.[10]

The responsibility for all these atrocities cannot be laid upon one organization alone, even a global one such as the United Nations. That said, it is the United Nations that enacted the Universal Declaration whose fiftieth anniversary we observe this year. This document suggests that the United Nations can and should assume the unique role of declaring and defending authentic human rights in the world. The dominance of the population control lobby there has, unfortunately, prevented it from doing so.

It is time for the United Nations to confront and combat this lobby and its dangerous ideology, which has proven itself so abusive of human dignity and human rights. Until the United Nations does this, those most in need of the Universal Declaration's protection and promises will consider it a *de facto* lie.

ENDNOTES

[1] There is every indication that it will, given the 1997 Beijing conference where officials unveiled more than 600 mobile abortion vans to provide abortion "services" to women.

[2] Bermudez, "Sterilization Without Consent," *Catholic World Report*, March 1998, pp. 42-44.

[3] Morrison, "Cutting the Poor," *Population Research Institute Review*, March/April 1998, p. 1.

[4] *Id.*

[5] When women were told of what was going on, tens of thousands simply refused to participate, bringing the project down.

[6] As documented first in *Reproductive Health Matters*, No. 6, November 1995, p. 85.

[7] *Id.*

[8] *The Human Laboratory*, BBC Documentary, November 1995.

[9] *Id.*

[10] U.N. Population Division, Conference, *Consequences and Policy Responses to Below-Replacement Fertility*, 6 November 1997.

Chapter 16

The United Nations, Feminism and Day Care: What Androgyny Means for Children

Babette Francis

The United Nations' mandate and commitment to promoting the well-being of children is being increasingly imperiled by some U.N. Conventions that cater to special interest groups rather than give priority to the most vulnerable section of humanity, the world's infants. These relatively recent Conventions are on a collision course with the Universal Declaration of Human Rights (UDHR), which, inspired by high ideals, was adopted by the member nations of the United Nations in 1948. Drafted in the aftermath of World War II, which caused tremendous suffering not only to active combatants but also to women and children, the 1948 UDHR asserted certain basic rights for all people.

Besides setting out fundamental freedoms and equality before the law, the Universal Declaration states unequivocally: "The family is the natural and fundamental group unit of society and is entitled to protection by society and the State" (Article 17), and "Motherhood and

Babette Francis, B. Sc. Hons. (Microbiology and Chemistry), is the mother of eight children and the national and overseas coordinator of Endeavour Forum, Inc., an Australian pro-life, pro-family lobby. She has attended and written on many U.N. conferences dealing with women's issues.

childhood are entitled to special care and assistance. All children, whether born in or out of wedlock, shall enjoy the same social protection" (Article 25).

The high ideals of the United Nations were maintained in its 1959 "Declaration on the Rights of the Child" that stated in Principle 6, *inter alia*: "A child of tender years shall not, save in exceptional circumstances, be separated from his mother."

However, by 1980, these high ideals appeared to have largely eroded. In July 1980, the United Nations "Convention on the Elimination of All Forms of Discrimination Against Women" (CEDAW)[1] was formally adopted at the United Nations Mid-Decade for Women World Conference in Copenhagen, and has been ratified by 161 countries. To date, fortunately, the U.S. Senate has not ratified this Treaty, despite the best efforts of the Clinton Administration, especially First Lady Hillary Clinton.

MOTHERHOOD AS SOCIAL FUNCTION

Like most U.N. Treaties, CEDAW enunciates many unexceptionable principles. However, while UDHR recognizes the special connection between mothers and children, CEDAW denies the difference between mothers and fathers and encourages mothers to work outside the home, ignoring the special need of infants for their mothers' presence. CEDAW's Articles 5 and 10 implicitly attack the special role of motherhood and raise concerns in the day-care debate.

Article 5 declares:

States Parties shall take all appropriate measures (a) To modify the social and cultural patterns of conduct of men and women, with a view to achieving the elimination of prejudices and customary and all other practices which are based on the idea of the inferiority or the superiority of either of the sexes or on stereotyped roles for men and women; [and] (b) To ensure that family education includes a proper understanding of maternity as a social function and the recognition of the common responsibility of men and women in the upbringing and development of their children, it being understood that the interest of the children is the primordial consideration in all cases.

The interpretation placed on Article 5(a) in many developed countries, including Australia and Canada, is that governments should be required to eliminate the traditional roles of men and women within the family (i.e., the concept of fathers being the main breadwinners while mothers are the primary caregivers for children). These are "stereotyped" roles and are not to be given social support, but instead are to be regarded as completely interchangeable.

Such a policy is further reinforced by Article 5(b), which requires family education to include a proper understanding of maternity as a "social function." To emphasize this concept overlooks maternity's biological significance—i.e., pregnancy, childbirth and, in particular, breastfeeding—because a "social function" in relation to the child is not exclusive to its mother but can be undertaken by any caregiver.

Article 10 of CEDAW deals with education, and Article 10(c) states that member nations "shall take all appropriate measures ... to ensure ... the elimination of any stereotyped concept of the roles of men and women at all levels and in all forms of education by encouraging co-education and other types of education which will help to achieve this aim and, in particular, by the revision of textbooks and school programs and the adaptation of teaching methods."

Thus, Article 5 of CEDAW promotes an androgynous view of humanity, or role reversal, among men and women, and Article 10 requires its implementation in education. In Australia, such "countersexism" has ranged from informal colored posters for kindergarten children showing a man bottle-feeding a baby while a woman climbs up a ladder to repair the roof, to the formal *Quality Improvement and Accreditation System Handbook*[2] that mandates what are considered anti-sexist procedures in day-care centers.

Australia was the first country in the world to develop a national child-care quality improvement system, initiated, funded and supported by the former Labor Government. Under Labor's policy, child-care centers that were not accredited would not be subsidized or granted operational costs. To achieve accreditation, centers had to adopt anti-sexist policies—e.g., staff could not provide "stereotyped toys such as trains, trucks and bulldozers for boys, or dolls and tea-sets for girls,"[3] nor should a staff member say to a little girl, "I love your pretty dress."[4] Breaches of these guidelines could incur denial or loss of accreditation, with the consequent loss of subsidies.

The American Association of University Women (AAUW) was well ahead of the field. At a workshop it held at the 1980 U.N. Mid-Decade for Women World Conference in Copenhagen, its representatives boasted about how they had eliminated "sexism" from U.S. textbooks. The AAUW decided to target California because that state is the largest purchaser of textbooks, and its members knew that if they won California, all the other publishers of textbooks would fall in line.

They gave an example of how they had gone through the elementary readers and eliminated a story about a little girl who, while playing in the garden, is frightened by a snake and runs in crying to her mother. Such a story was unacceptable, as it showed a female who was both fearful and tearful (and had a mother at home to attend to her fears and tears). At this workshop, I suggested that it was sensible for a girl to be afraid of snakes, as they are potentially deadly, but the AAUW insisted the story had to be deleted. My jest that such censorship was not eliminating sexism but indulging in "snakeism," i.e., discrimination against snakes, was not appreciated.[5]

Insofar as childhood play is a form of preparation for adult life, a little girl who is not allowed to play with dolls may feel some trepidation in handling her own infant later on. Memories of the toy bulldozer with which she was confronted in the day-care center are hardly likely to be helpful. Fortunately, nature is not so easily fooled, and many little girls have been observed treating their toy trucks as if they were baby carriages.

A DENIAL OF ITS OWN POLICY

The denial of the unique significance of motherhood is the United Nations' most serious betrayal of infants and puts it into direct conflict with its own health policy. To do the United Nations justice, both its health agency, the World Health Organization (WHO), and the United Nations International Children's Emergency Fund (UNICEF) have consistently and vigorously promoted the breastfeeding of infants.

In 1979, WHO and UNICEF jointly convened a landmark meeting in Geneva on the feeding of infants and young children. The meeting's recommendations on breastfeeding and "an international code of marketing" on artificial formula were unanimously endorsed by the World Health Assembly in resolution WHA33.32.[6] In 1990, the "Innocenti Declaration on the Protection, Promotion and Support of Breastfeeding" was adopted by participants at a WHO/UNICEF policymakers' meeting on "Breastfeeding in the 1990s: A Global Initiative." The meeting, cosponsored by the U.S. Agency for International Development (USAID) and the Swedish International Development Authority (SIDA), declared:

> As a global goal for optimal maternal and child health and nutrition, all women should be enabled to practice exclusive breastfeeding and all infants should be fed exclusively on breast milk from birth to 4-6 months of age. Thereafter children should continue to breastfeed, while

receiving appropriate and adequate complementary foods, for up to two years or beyond. This child feeding ideal is to be achieved by creating an appropriate environment of awareness and support so that women can breastfeed in this manner. Attainment of the goal requires, in many countries, the reinforcement of a 'breastfeeding culture' and its vigorous defence against incursions of a 'bottle-feeding culture.' This requires commitment and advocacy for social mobilisation, utilizing to the full the prestige and authority of acknowledged leaders of society in all walks of life.[7]

WHO and UNICEF cite the benefits of breastfeeding not only to infants in terms of superior nutrition, reduced infections, and allergies, but also to women in reducing the risk of breast and ovarian cancers.

The United Nations' breastfeeding policy was confirmed in 1996 at the 49th World Health Assembly with a resolution (WHA49/15) that stated: "Member states reaffirm the recommendation of about 6 months of exclusive breastfeeding, and continued breastfeeding with complementary foods such as those from the local family diet continuing from 6 months to 2 years."[8]

Breastfeeding Management in Australia states, "Unrestricted access to the breast is crucial to establishing lactation without problems."[9] Such unrestricted access to the mother cannot be achieved if the baby is left in day care all day. Some "supermoms" manage for a while to breastfeed by ingenious scheduling or by expressing milk, storing it in the fridge and transporting it to the day-care center, but few infants who are routinely left in day care are exclusively breastfed for six months, let alone breastfed for two years and beyond.

If not for its obsession with the androgyny of male/female roles, the United Nations might have advised that its admirable health goals in regard to infants could be achieved through maternity leave, paid or unpaid, followed by mothers' judicious involvement in part-time jobs as their infants grew older, or, with the aid of the new information technology, by career work from the home that did not involve separation from their babies. However, with feminist ideologues prevailing at the United Nations, there will not be any acknowledgment that the career paths of men and women can be different, and indeed should be different for the optimum care of infants.

In the Third World, many mothers routinely take their infants to work with them in the fields. This is not ideal, but it is far preferable to the alternative of someone else feeding the infant with artificial formula prepared with possibly unsafe water. U.N. Conventions that attempt to break the connection between mothers and infants can be lethal for the latter in a Third World context.

The actual implementation of the admirable WHO/UNICEF resolutions on breastfeeding seems to be directed more toward targeting and attacking the marketers of artificial formula[10] than toward emphasizing a mother's unique and irreplaceable role in caring for her preschool children. In Geneva, on August 11, 1998, Gro Harlem Bruntland, new head of WHO, called on the pediatric profession to guard against aggressive marketing of breastmilk substitutes. However, no similar caution against leaving infants in day care was made.

DISCRIMINATION AGAINST STAY-AT-HOME MOMS

The new androgyny and the United Nations' promotion of women's participation in the paid workforce, with the consequent growth in the child-care industry, have been adopted as government policy in developed countries, with taxpayer subsidies to centers where infants are cared for by strangers. Combined with tax penalties for single-income families, such policies cause major financial problems for mothers who wish to remain out of the paid workforce to care for their children. In Australia, many surveys have shown that the majority of mothers with preschool children would prefer to do this while their children are young, and that many who have full-time jobs would prefer to work part-time.[11] However, their preferences have been ignored by successive governments. In the recent federal election campaign, Labor Opposition Leader Mr. Kim Beazley declaimed, "Our policy is to get women back to work"—as if what women did in the home was not work and was of no value.[12]

Government policies have been similar in other developed countries, particularly Canada, which has enthusiastically ratified CEDAW. Ironically, a Canadian housewife lodged a complaint with the United Nations itself about discrimination against full-time homemakers. Mrs. Beverley Smith's complaint against the Canadian government, citing 12 grounds of discrimination, was dealt with by the Working Group of the U.N. Commission on the Status of Women in March 1999.[13] The three grounds relevant to day care were as follows:

1.   There is discrimination in the tax law that does not permit women who work in the home to be paid a salary by their husbands or to

have any money allotted for unemployment, sick benefits or other benefits for which all other workers are eligible.[14]

2.   There is discrimination in the tax law that results in a married man and woman being taxed more heavily if they have a single income rather than dual income, despite having the same total income and number of dependents.[15] (This discrimination is similar to the "marriage tax penalty" in the United States and to the discrimination against single-income families in Australia, who are entitled to only one tax-free threshold of $5,400, whereas in two-income families, each wage earner benefits from the tax-free threshold, so that the couple can earn $10,800 tax-free, even if the total family income is the same in both cases).

3.   There is discrimination in the tax law that allows a woman who puts her child into care by a stranger or a nanny to deduct the expenses of this care, up to $6,000 per child per year, to age 14, while a mother who opts for any other child-care arrangement may not deduct expenses. The tax system therefore discriminates against the option of having a child cared for by a blood relative, including a grandmother, a friend, a sibling, or even one of the parents.[16]

Mrs. Smith's case was decided with the following general determination: "The Working Group expressed its deep concern in relation to violations of economic, social and cultural rights, and the pervasive discrimination against women." Though vague, the determination was a victory of sorts for Mrs. Smith, because it induced the Canadian government to have its ministers meet with her to discuss her concerns.

An Australian pro-family organization, Endeavour Forum, Inc., has lodged a similar complaint against the Australian government.[17] Child-care subsidies to mothers who place their children in day care can be over $60 per week, even to couples with a joint annual income over $70,000. In contrast, mothers who care for their own children get less than $30, and even that is cut back if annual family income exceeds $30,000.

Beverley Smith's complaint was supported by over 20 national organizations around the world. It should be noted that the United Nations' processing of her claim proceeded at a glacial pace, as that of Endeavour Forum is now doing, whereas the United Nations appears to deal promptly with complaints of discrimination by homosexual groups or indigenous minorities.

WHO and UNICEF have done some good work in regard to children's health, but much of it is likely to be negated by the health risks incurred by young children in day care. John Bowlby,[18] Selma Fraiberg,[19] Penelope Leach[20] and others have written on the consequences, including emotional risks, failure to bond, and developmental problems, of separating infants from their mothers.

In a 1994 *Medical Journal of Australia* article on the risk of infections in group day care, M. J. Ferson states:

> Recent reports have documented increased risks of infectious illness among children in group day care, their family contacts and the staff caring for them. Children who attend group care have more episodes of upper respiratory and middle-ear infections, pneumonia, and gastroenteritis than children cared for at home. They are also at increased risk of life-threatening infections by Haemophilus influenza type B. Conditions which commonly affect adult contacts include upper respiratory tract infections, hepatitis A, cytomegalovirus (CMV), enteric infections such as giardia, rotavirus and shigella, and skin infections and infestations.[21]

A Norwegian study has found that toddlers who attend day care are twice as likely to develop asthma,[22] and Dr. Leslee Roberts of Australian National University warned an international conference on respiratory infections that toddlers in day care developed six more infections per year than those cared for at home. Other delegates warned against babies under the age of one being placed in day care because they have weak immune systems.[23] The official recommendation of the American Academy of Pediatrics is that children under two should be cared for only with their own brothers and sisters.

Australian psychologist and bestselling author Steve Biddulph also has had the courage to challenge the prevailing politically correct view on child care. In his 1994 book, *More Secrets of Happy Children*, Biddulph writes that it is his belief that regular day care for children under three will result in these children having a seriously deprived childhood experience. The younger the children and the more hours they spend in an institutional setting, the more serious will be their deprivation. The mental and physical health of these children is likely to be affected, and they may have difficulty bonding with and caring for their own children. In addition, mothers who put their young children in child-care centers may suffer high levels of depression.[24]

So overwhelming is the evidence against the long-term placement of infants in day care that feminist psychologist L.B. Silverstein has pleaded for "a cessation of the research agenda that searches for negative consequences of non-parental care and maternal employment."[25] This is akin to and allied with feminist pleas for an end to the study of sex differences, a political censorship of research.[26]

Ultimately, we cannot lay all the blame on the United Nations, many of whose member nations are developing countries that do not readily facilitate radical feminist goals. The real threat comes from feminist bureaucrats and feminist non-governmental organizations (NGOs) from the developed world, notably Canada, the United States and the European Union, that push the feminist agenda at U.N. conferences. Because of the financial clout of their "donor" nations with regard to development loans from the World Bank, the IMF and aid agencies, they are able to coerce the representatives of developing nations into supporting the feminist agenda. At the United Nations Habitat II World Conference in Istanbul in 1996, Michael Cohen, representing the World Bank, confirmed that the interest rates on some loans to developing countries were contingent on these countries' adoption of some aspects of the feminist agenda imposed on them by Western donors.

The process works in a circular way: Feminist NGOs are given accreditation and privileged access to the inner workings of the United Nations, while pro-family organizations are cold-shouldered. For example, Catholics for a Free Choice, the pro-abortion lobby that has few members but receives large donations from wealthy foundations in the United States, has been accredited by the United Nations, whereas Human Life International, which has a large, active membership and branches all over the world, has been denied accreditation. Once accredited, feminist NGOs appear to be given a free hand to attend key meetings, to make their voices heard, and in some circumstances even to draft significant United Nations documents.[27]

The late Bella Abzug's Women's Environment and Development Organization (WEDO) is a classic example of an NGO that is given such privileged access, as is the Women's Caucus of the NGOs. These organizations are so influential that they appear to be the coordinators of the NGO Forums that are held in conjunction with official United Nations conferences. The influence of Canadian organizations, such as the Commission on the Status of Women and the Montreal-based International Center for Human Rights and Democratic Development, are also all-pervasive. Western feminists seem to believe that women in the developing world are suffering from a kind of sexual false consciousness that needs attention from the more enlightened.

The underlying ideology is that of the National Organization for Women (NOW), articulated by Wilma Scott Heide: "Unless women have, from the moment of birth, socialization for, expectations of, and preparation for a viable significant alternative to motherhood ... women will continue to want and reproduce too many children."[28] A more extreme example is author Jesse Bernard's suggestion: "Perhaps girls could be given an electric shock whenever they see a picture of an adorable baby until the very thought of motherhood becomes anathema to them."[29]

CONCLUSION

In his 1996 seminal work, *Early Child Care: Infants and Nations At Risk,* Australian child psychiatrist Peter Cook writes:

> National policies are needed which lead to community and legislative recognition that children in the first three to five years of life, especially infants, and also their mothers, form a discrete and vulnerable group with special and important needs. ... It is lamentable that the strength of the movement against full-time mothering has led to a situation where it is sometimes not politically correct to say publicly that the mother is the best person to look after her baby or young child.[30]

However, there is a whiff of change in the air. Norway has paved the way to developing a national policy in favor of mothering by proposing to pay parents $600 a month provided they do not use a public day-care center.[31] There have been the predictable howls of protest from feminists who see this as yet another ploy to force women back into the kitchen, rather than seeing it as offering a choice. The proposed payment is not putting a price tag on the work of mothers—it is merely restoring some equity to the tax system. All families are heavily taxed to provide day-care centers; the payment to families who do not use day care is offering them the chance to make alternative arrangements. The Australian Liberal-National Party Coalition Government, in its tax reform package due to be implemented in the year 2000, has also moved to eliminate some of the taxation injustices inflicted on single-income families in which the mother remains out of the paid workforce to care for her children.[32] The Australian government has had the courage to do this despite criticism from the U.N. CEDAW Committee for cuts to child care and to the budget of the Office of the Status of Women—and it won the October 1998 Federal election.

If other countries are inspired to adopt similar policies, the new millennium may usher in a brighter future for the world's children.

ENDNOTES

[1] The U.N. Convention on the Elimination of All Forms of Discrimination against Women was opened for signature on March 1, 1980; the Convention entered into force on September 3, 1981. As of April 15, 1984, 56 countries had consented to be bound by its provisions, through either ratification or accession. The number of countries bound currently is 161.

[2] National Child Care Accreditation Council, *Quality Improvement and Accreditation System Handbook: Putting Children First* (Canberra, Australia: 1993).

[3] *Ibid.*, Principle 3, p. 9.

[4] *Ibid.*, Principle 19, p. 65.

[5] "The Myth of Consensus: UN Decade for Women," *QUADRANT*, December 1980, p. 22.

[6] *The Code Handbook—A Guide to Implementing the International Code of Marketing of Breastmilk Substitutes,* (New York: WHO/UNICEF), 1979.

[7] *Innocenti Declaration on the Protection, Promotion and Support of Breastfeeding*, WHO/UNICEF, August 1, 1990, Florence, Italy.

[8] *A Guide to Implementing the International Code of Marketing of Breastmilk Substitutes* (New York: UNICEF, June 1996), Appendix C, Nutrition Section.

[9] Nursing Mothers of Association of Australia, *Breastfeeding Management in Australia*, ed. Wendy Brodribb (Merrily Enterprises Pty. Ltd., 1990).

[10] "Child Poverty Deaths," *The (Melbourne) Herald Sun*, August 12, 1998.

[11] Audrey Vandenheuvel, "Mothers with young children," *Family Matters*, December 30, 1991, pp. 47-49; Michelle Grattan, "Young mothers should stay home poll," *The Age*, Student Update, Melbourne, November 13, 1995; and Michelle Pountney, "Working mums out of favour," *The (Melbourne) Herald Sun*, December 13, 1997, p. 10.

[12] Opposition Leader's federal election launch speech, September 1998.

[13] Complaint dated May 27, 1997, by Mrs. Beverley Smith, Calgary, Canada, to the United Nations, re: discrimination by Canadian government against full-time homemakers.

[14] *Boland v. Minister of National Revenue*, Income Tax Court of Canada: 93 D.T.C. 1558 T.C.C.

[15] Mr. Michael Walter, Fraser Institute Report, 1996.

[16] *Boland v. Minister of National Revenue, op. cit.*

[17] Complaint dated December 1, 1997, by Endeavour Forum, Australia, to the United Nations, re: discrimination by Australian Government against full-time homemakers.

[18] J. Bowlby, *Maternal Care and Mental Health* (World Health Organization: 1951); *also* J. Bowlby, *Attachment and Loss,* Vol. 1, *Attachment* (New York: Basic Books, 1969), p. xii, and Vol. 2, *Separation Anxiety and Anger* (New York: Basic Books, 1973).

[19] Selma Fraiberg, *Every Child's Birthright—In Defence of Mothering* (New York: Bantam Books, 1978).

[20] Penelope Leach, *Children First* (London: Michael Joseph, 1994).

[21] M.J. Ferson, "Control of infections in child care," *Medical Journal of Australia* 161: 615-618.

[22] "Asthma linked to child centers," *The (Melbourne) Herald Sun*, September 25, 1997.

[23] Andrew Cummins, "Toddlers in care risk more colds," *The (Melbourne) Herald Sun*, July 28, 1997.

[24] Steve Biddulph, *More Secrets of Happy Children* (Sydney, Australia: Bay Books, an imprint of HarperCollins Publishers, 1994), pp. 68, 72.

[25] L.B. Silverstein, "Transforming the debate about child care and maternal employment," *American Psychologist* 46 (1991): 1025-1032.

[26] Deborah L. Rhode, ed., *Theoretical Perspectives on Sexual Differences* (outgrowth of a conference sponsored by Stanford's Institute of Research on Women and Gender in 1987; subjects included feminist theory, sex differences, sex roles; Dewey Number 305.4201 THE) and Rachel T. Hare-Martin and Jeanne Marecek, eds., *Making a Difference: Psychology and the Construction of Gender* (subjects and sex roles and women psychology; Bib Record ID 00 6640550 Dewey Number 305 3H 275M), both published by Yale University, 1990.

[27] Human Life International Special Report No. 163, July 1998, p. 7.

[28] Wilma Scott Heide, former chairman of the board of directors, National Organization for Women, cited by Allan Carlson in "Reflections on the American Social Crisis," *Family Questions* (New Brunswick, N.J.: Transaction Books, 1998), p. 8.

[29] Jesse Bernard, "The Future of Motherhood," 1974, cited by Maggie Gallagher in *Enemies of Eros: How the Sexual Revolution is Killing Family, Marriage and Sex and What We Can Do About It* (Chicago: Bonus Books, 1989).

[30] Peter S. Cook, "Early Child Care: Infants and Nations at Risk (Melbourne: News Weekly Books, 1997), p. 154.

[31] "Child-care war," *The (Melbourne) Herald Sun*, February 26, 1998.

[32] "Tax Reform, not a new tax," Australian government booklet mailed to all households, August 1998. *See also* website taxreform.gov.au.

Chapter 17

Human Rights and U.S. Military Interventions

Karl Farris

The year 1998 witnessed numerous declarations, speeches, meetings and conferences celebrating the fiftieth anniversary of the Universal Declaration of Human Rights that was passed by the General Assembly of the United Nations in 1948. The intent was to establish international norms for how states must treat their own citizens. It was hoped that universally recognized civil political, social and economic rights would further the cause of international peace.

Skeptics, however, saw the Declaration as little more than a collection of pious phrases, since the long accepted principle of state sovereignty held that whatever states did to their own citizens was no one else's business.[1] Indeed, throughout most of the Cold War period, the world at large remained oblivious to the Declaration and its human rights provisions.

The end of the Cold War, though welcomed, unleashed a period of violent conflicts. Many of these occurred within states where human

Karl Farris, Colonel, U.S. Army (Ret.), was an Armor officer on active duty for 30 years, serving in various command and staff assignments in the United States, Europe and southeast Asia. In 1993, he established the U.S. Army Peacekeeping Institute and served as its first director, from 1993 until 1996.

rights were generally ignored or deliberately violated. In fact, the majority of casualties in these conflicts have been, and continue to be, not active combatants but civilians. Citing a humanitarian obligation to come to the aid of threatened populations and spurred on by non-governmental organizations (NGOs) that promote human rights, the United Nations has aggressively intervened in these internal state conflicts under the guise of "peacekeeping" and "humanitarian assistance."[2]

While these post-Cold War interventions continue to be called *peacekeeping*, they are really new types of interventions. No peace ever exists before the "peacekeepers" are dispatched. These intrusive interventions bear little resemblance to the largely benign peacekeeping operations conducted during the Cold War period. Instead, they are "muscular," requiring large numbers of military forces.

Possessing the world's strongest and most capable military, the United States is becoming ever more involved in this type of global "peacekeeping" and humanitarian action. Cumulatively, these operations have had a significant negative impact on the readiness of U.S. military forces for combat, which remains their primary duty.

U.S. MILITARY READINESS

Over the past few years, most of the key components of the U.S. military's readiness (personnel, training and equipment) have steadily deteriorated. A *U.S. News and World Report* investigative report on the state of America's military forces posed the question "Can Peacekeepers Make War?"[3] This question was prompted by mounting evidence that our military's conventional combat skills and the warrior ethic that goes with them were being eroded by a combination of downsizing, budget cuts, and widespread commitment to non-combat operations in the Balkans, the Middle East and elsewhere. The investigative reporters found that non-combat missions such as peacekeeping and humanitarian efforts "are diluting the warfighting capability of U.S. troops by disrupting combat training and breaking down unit cohesion."[4]

The simple truth is that America's military force is busier than ever, despite being 36 percent smaller and suffering a 40 percent budget decline since the end of the Cold War.[5] What's more, the United States is increasingly using its forces for missions not related to their primary purpose: the defense and security of their nation through military force, or war. Instead, the dramatic increase is in what the military calls "Operations Other Than War" (OOTW), which is to say, peacekeeping and humanitarian assistance. The net result is that the U.S. military currently finds itself working harder and longer with fewer people and fewer spare parts, and spending more time deployed overseas.

The situation is rapidly reaching a crisis point. One telling example is the plummeting retention rates for Army pilots. One hundred percent manning rates for Army helicopter pilots were long the norm. These have now fallen to 85 percent. When asked, helicopter pilots attribute this significant attrition partly to the open-ended mission in the Balkans, which sees them returning to Europe after only 24 months in the United States and then serving one-half to two-thirds of their three years in Europe as part of the peacekeeping mission in Bosnia.[6]

President Clinton met with the nation's top military leaders at Fort McNair in Washington, D.C., on September 15, 1998, specifically to address the military's growing concern about readiness. At that meeting, the leaders told the president that "shortfalls were eroding their readiness to fight and win the next war. This includes shortages of spare parts for warplanes, cuts in training and difficulties in recruiting and keeping qualified troops."[7]

Most military leaders will admit that a significant portion of the military's current readiness problems can be attributed directly to the increased involvement in peacekeeping and other non-warfighting related operations such as humanitarian assistance. The higher operational tempo caused by these deployments wears out equipment faster, causing a need for more funding for spare parts, and increases deployment time for soldiers, affecting retention rates.

In this regard, the current U.S. military commitment in Bosnia is instructive and provides a glimpse into the future if the United States keeps going down this road. The U.S. military involvement in Bosnia was scheduled for one year. The cost estimate was $1.5 billion. The commitment has now become open-ended, and expenses surpassed $7 billion in April 1998.[8]

ASSAULT ON STATE SOVEREIGNTY

While there is now a growing awareness of the declining ability of America's military to effectively and efficiently fight and win the nation's wars, others view the use of the U.S. military for such non-combat-related tasks and missions as both logical and desirable. They claim that we face no "peer" military competitor as we did, arguably, with the Soviet military during the Cold War.[9]   And, they contend, because of our current dominant position in the world, we have a unique opportunity and responsibility in concert with international organizations and other transnational actors to begin to right many of the world's wrongs.   This should include, they argue, the use of our military to assist and advance the cause of democracy and human rights.

Such a view continues to be pushed by humanitarian aid officials who believe that the U.S. military has little to do in the post-Cold War world. They argue that the military can be used for projects not related to American security but aiming to further the "common cause of man" in a now interdependent world.

This one-world, global interdependency focus first surfaced among modernists in the 1970s who predicted the demise of sovereignty and the traditional nation-state. They claimed that the communications and information revolutions would eliminate both.   In their places would emerge non-territorial actors such as multinational corporations, transnational social movements and international organizations.   They characterized this emerging world as an interconnected "global village," where internal state matters would become a thing of the past. (However, these same NGOs also pressure multinational companies to review specific nations' human rights records when selecting countries in which to do business.   They also actively push for human rights in the countries where such companies currently operate.)

The concept of a "global village" is in direct contravention to the United Nations charter, which recognizes the absolute sovereignty of all nations. Article 2, Section 7 of the charter specifically protects sovereign member states from any outside involvement in their domestic affairs.

Despite this, leaders of the United Nations continue to denigrate the concept of state sovereignty, encouraged by internationalists espousing a "one world government." In a June 1992 landmark document titled *An Agenda for Peace*, then United Nations Secretary-General Boutros Boutros-Ghali declared, "[T]he time of absolute and exclusive sovereignty has passed."[10]   In its place, he called for an expanded U.N. role in the world. Among the changes he desired was the right to intervene in the internal affairs of sovereign states in the name of those states' citizens' human rights.[11]

The bottom line was that U.N. Secretary-General Boutros-Ghali wanted the United Nations to recognize the principle that violations of human rights within a sovereign state could be viewed as constituting the existence of a threat or breach of the peace. Such a finding would give the United Nations the right to call on its member nations to intervene with military forces in internal state matters, ostensibly to protect the "universal" human rights of any country's citizens.

It should be noted that Chapter VII of the United Nations' Charter already authorizes the Security Council to determine the existence of a threat or breach of the peace or act of aggression and to make recommendations or decide on measures of a mandatory character to restore and maintain the peace. This may include economic and diplomatic sanctions or a broad range of military actions. U.N. member states are required by the U.N. Charter to carry out decisions of the Council. It is unclear what Boutros-Ghali's proposal would add to this, other than increased authorization for intrusion into the internal affairs of sovereign states on ever shakier grounds.

While understandable, his view creates its own problems, not least of which is the extensive disagreement on what actually constitutes a human right, or human rights abuses.[12] For the purposes of this paper, the specific difficulty is the compromise of national sovereignty of the allegedly offending nation, as well as the undefined obligation of human rights-enforcing member nations. These obstacles are not insurmountable, but they are obstacles nonetheless and should be recognized as such. Only then can we establish a coherent and compelling policy that will allow for military intervention in the right cases.

INEFFICACY OF RECENT INTRA-STATE INTERVENTIONS

Heavily influenced by "one-world" thinking, the United Nations quickly became mired in costly and complex political-military operations in Cambodia, Somalia, the former Yugoslavia, and Haiti. These were launched in rapid succession without any clear understanding of, consensus on or doctrine for the use of military forces in states plagued by civil conflict. The missions in Somalia and the former Yugoslavia proved to be outright failures, with the United Nations leaving in disgrace. After missions in Cambodia and Haiti, both touted by the United Nations as successful, the populations today are suffering as much political, social, and economic dislocation and human rights abuses as they did before the costly U.N. interventions.

From an operational standpoint, the record of recent U.N. interventions is filled with instances of ineptitude in the field, problems of coordination and cooperation among the mission's various components, and outright failures of leadership.

What these examples have shown is that these costly military-led humanitarian interventions are a high-risk, short-term, and imperfect strategy. Even NATO's muscular "peacekeeping" operation in Bosnia, which followed the United Nations' failed three-and-a-half-year effort (called UNPROFOR) in that country, is far from making any real headway. Today, few of the Bosnians internally displaced in the name of "ethnic cleansing" have been allowed to return to their homes if these are in areas controlled by another ethnic group. More ominous, the Bosnian election results released by international officials on September 25, 1998, confirmed the victory of extreme nationalist candidate Nikola Poplasen for president of the Bosnian Serb half of the country. This is widely seen as a serious setback for the Western strategy of supporting cooperative and less nationalistic politicians.

So four years after the Dayton Agreement, instead of the envisioned multi-ethnic state, Bosnia remains divided into three ethnic enclaves, functioning only because a quasi-Western protectorate has been established. Prospects for Kosovo look no better.

What has been learned from the humanitarian-inspired interventions in Somalia, Cambodia, Haiti and Bosnia is that "neither a UN[-]led military operation nor United States military power can impose on local conflicts any long-lasting solutions that deviate from the realities of local power."[13] Nevertheless, these largely ineffective but resource-draining ventures continue to be pushed by those who believe that their goals are politically possible just because they are morally desirable.[14]

THE U.S. MILITARY SHOULD REMAIN TRAINED AND READY FOR FIGHTING WARS—NOT FOR "GLOBAL GENDARMERIE" TASKS

What is the responsibility of United Nations and more specifically the United States, as leader of the free world, in this difficult post-Cold War period when large areas of the globe seem to be on the verge of massive dislocation?

First, the principles of state sovereignty and the primacy of the nation-state, which have been the very foundation of international relations for more than 300 years, should be reaffirmed. Articles 15(1) and 28 of the Universal Declaration of Human Rights states, "Everyone has the right to a nationality"; and "Everyone is entitled to a social and international order in which the rights and freedoms set forth in this Declaration can be fully realized." These two articles taken together affirm the legitimacy and primacy of nation-states and national sovereignty, as well as allow for the occasional need for nation-states to contribute to international order through multilateral cooperation.

Second, we must recognize that neither the United Nations nor any other international organization can effectively act in the place of the nation-state. As Ambassador Edward Marks observed in a paper entitled *UN Peacekeeping in a post-Cold War World*: "The United Nations ... is not really a single political or bureaucratic institution with a distinctive character or personality, much less independent authority. Most specifically it is not a government and does not react like one."[15] The United Nations and other international institutions cannot be autonomous actors. They are organizations intended to facilitate cooperation among sovereign states.

Third, we must acknowledge that the sovereign nation-state has proven to be more resilient than the modernists had predicted, and that the "New World Order" has simply not emerged. Nation-states continue to receive the loyalties of the vast majority of the world's people.   This is an excellent trend, since history shows that strong nation-states based on the democratic model offer the best protection for human rights. As a 1997 Carnegie Commission report on "Preventing Deadly Conflict" concluded, "[C]apable states with representative governance based on the rule of law" provide the best guarantee for the "protection of fundamental human rights."[16]

Finally, we must acknowledge that employing American military might indiscriminately in humanitarian interventions and nation-building ventures ultimately threatens the readiness of those same military forces to which the world looks for maintenance of international security and for truly protecting and furthering the cause of universal human rights. Though the Clinton administration's policy has usually violated this principle, its National Security Strategy, published in May 1997, at least voices it, stating:

> [W]e know there must be limits to America's involvement in the world. We must be selective in the use of our capabilities, and the choice we make always must be guided by advancing our objectives of a more secure, prosperous, and free America. ... [T]he goal of the national security strategy is to ensure the protection of our nation's fundamental and enduring needs.[17]

Many factors will influence America's decisions about when, why and how to use military force. But the key factor must remain its national interest. A strong and ready American military is necessary for the preservation of America's national sovereignty and to help support and defend the sovereignty of those democratic nations that respect the human rights of their citizens. In the long run, this will contribute more to furthering the cause of human rights across the globe than fashionable crusading impulses.

ENDNOTES

[1] David Manasian, "A Survey of Human-Rights Law: The World is Watching," *The Economist,* Dec. 5-11, 1998, pp. 1-16.

[2] It is interesting to note that governments with clout can generally avoid criticism for their human rights records in the United Nations. The U.N. Commission on Human Rights, which regularly criticizes individual countries for their human rights records, has never passed a resolution criticizing China's human rights record, even after the Tiananmen Square massacre.

[3] Richard J. Newman, "Can Peacekeepers Make War?" in *U.S. News & World Report,* Jan. 19, 1998, pp. 39-44.

[4] *Ibid.,* p. 3. These findings are also supported in several United States General Accounting Office reports, such as Peace Operations: Heavy Use of Key Capabilities May Affect Response to Regional Conflicts (GAO/NSIAD-95-51) Peace Operations: Effect of Training, Equipment, and Other Factors on Unit Capability (GAO/NSIAD-96-14), and *U.N. Peacekeeping: Status of Long-standing Operations and U.S. Interest in Supporting Them* (GAO/NSIAD-97-59).

[5] William S. Cohen, "Defense: Getting Down to Basics," *The Washington Post,* April 22, 1998, p. A23.

[6] Chuck Vineh, "Army Battles Pilot Shortage Head-On," *Pacific Stars & Stripes,* April 7, 1998.

[7] Steven Lee Myers, "More Money for Readiness: Military Wins Budget Pledge from Clinton," *Wilmington Morning Star,* September 23, 1998, p. 3A.

[8] Charles William Maynes, "The Perils of (and for) an Imperial America," *Foreign Policy,* Summer 1998, p. 37.

[9] The Cold War U.S. military focus on maintaining a high warfighting readiness paid off in the 1991 Gulf War when the U.S. military quickly defeated a sizeable and battle-tested Iraqi army with minimal cost in American lives.

[10] Boutros Boutros-Ghali, *An Agenda for Peace: Preventive Diplomacy, Peacemaking and Peacekeeping,* Report of the Secretary-General Pursuant to the Statement Adopted by the Summit Meeting of the Security Council on January 31, 1992 (New York City, N.Y.: United Nations, 1992).

[11] *Ibid.*

[12] *See,* for example, the other essays in this paper series.

[13] Samuel P. Huntington, "The West Unique, Not Universal," *Foreign Affairs,* Nov./Dec. 1996, p. 42.

[14] Ernest W. Lefever, *The Irony of Virtue: Ethics and American Power* (Boulder, Colo.: Westview Press, 1998), p. 215.

[15] Edward Marks and William Lewis, *Triage for Failing States*, McNair Paper (Washington, D.C.: Institute for National Strategic Studies, National Defense University Press, 1994), p. 26.

[16] Manasian, *op. cit.*, p. 1.

[17] President William J. Clinton, "A National Security Strategy for a New Century," The 1997 National Security Strategy Report, forwarded to Congress May 15, 1997.

Chapter 18

Reflections of an Ambassador

Alan Keyes

Despite the dangerous flaws in the conception and development of the United Nations' vision of global unity, it is important to remember that the effort itself began during the closing days and aftermath of the Second World War. At the end of such a period of exhausting war and wickedness, it was natural that there would be a great desire to relieve the world of the possibility of its happening again. The nations that originally formed the United Nations were those that had just heroically spent themselves in the struggle to defeat international evil. We should be slow to criticize their decent impulse to use that moment of great moral focus to lay a foundation of common action that would prevent the return of the unimaginable evils they had just seen. The Charter of the United Nations states that one of the basic purposes of the organization is "promoting and encouraging respect for human rights and for fundamental freedoms for all without distinction as to race, sex, language, or religion."

On December 10, 1948, the General Assembly of the United Nations adopted and proclaimed the Universal Declaration of Human Rights— the subject of this series of papers. Much as the Declaration of

Alan Keyes, Ph.D., is a former U.S. ambassador to the United Nations Economic and Social Council and Assistant Secretary of State for International Organizational Affairs.

Independence did in the American context, the Universal Declaration of Human Rights has come to epitomize the effort of the United Nations to advance the cause of human dignity in the world.

The fiftieth anniversary of the Universal Declaration is an appropriate time to evaluate that effort. This series considers the progress that has been made by the United Nations in advancing the universal cause of human rights and human dignity. These essays provide an extensive overview of the state of the project begun with such high hopes half a century ago. And while it is important always to look with charity on the good intentions of that project, it is actually well past time that we took stock of the real effect it has had on the people it was intended to serve.

The papers in this series make it clear that the United Nations has failed to advance the cause of human dignity in the world. This failure is particularly marked in precisely those areas that involve the attempt to translate the general language of the Universal Declaration into concrete respect for human rights. On issue after issue, these papers tell the sorry story of the impotence and even the active complicity of the United Nations in the systematic suppression of both understanding of and respect for those rights. Like accumulating symptoms that point undeniably to some hidden cause of physical illness, so the record of the United Nations in advancing human rights is a list of the symptoms of a fundamental corruption in the effort itself.

We need to ask the causes of this failure, because we need to learn from it. Whatever the eventual fate of the United Nations, the effort to advance the universal cause of justice will continue, and it is particularly important that the United States and its citizens take an intelligent and effective part in it. That means that we must understand the root cause of what has gone wrong with the United Nations.

That cause is actually quite clear. The founders of the United Nations failed to take account of moral reality. It never was to be expected that the institution could effectively respect principles of decency and right when it was from the beginning substantially composed of nations that do not base their own practice on principles of decency and right.

Consider, as perhaps the most prominent example, the role of the Marxist Soviet Union in the United Nations. For much of the postwar era, the Soviet Union was the principal impediment to the effective defense of human rights around the world. The Soviets were wholly outside of and opposed to the tradition of respect for human dignity to which the United Nations was supposedly devoted.

But the Soviets acted in bad faith not simply because they were wicked, but because Marxism is materialist in principle and denies the distinct nature of man. The Marxist view is intrinsically opposed to the doctrine of human rights and to the doctrine of eternal justice that underlies it. Man is just an extension of the material world, in the Marxist view, and so all professions of respect for human distinctness are in bad faith in principle, because ultimately the only thing a consistent Marxist will respect is the power of matter unfolding itself in history. Soviet disrespect for moral truth was no secret to the founders of the United Nations. And the decision to form an organization that included such a nation is the clearest possible sign that right belief on moral matters was never a defining characteristic of the community being formed.

So the United Nations fails with respect to human rights because it is based on a false practical principle—it does not take seriously the requirement of moral principle in politics. This is not just an incidental failure. It is a failure that derives from a fundamentally wrong understanding of politics—from the view that there can be a political whole that is not ultimately rooted in a community of moral belief. No procedural or organizational cleverness can bring tyrannical countries together with principled ones to form a group that respects human liberty.

The naïve expectation that this could be pulled off is not just a case of excessive optimism in the founders of the United Nations. It also reveals a fundamental inclination to accept the social science vision of politics—that politics is ultimately about the patterns of organization that will emerge from mankind's material and instinctive nature. In this view, moral principle and claims of truth and justice are simply manifestations of the deeper material structure of human nature.

Because the membership of the United Nations from the beginning included nations that denied the real foundations of respect for human dignity, it is not surprising that the Universal Declaration of Human Rights would also betray ambiguity at critical moments. Although defenders of the document have worked hard to characterize it as a prudent expression of an implied doctrine of natural law with an ultimate foundation in the God of nature, the fact is that the document is an ungrounded moral façade—moral injunctions floating free of any principled reason that would require assent, and thus moral words without a corresponding soul.

The first article of the Universal Declaration makes reference to the rational nature of all men, and this is indeed one of the paths to understanding that the God of nature has willed that human beings be accorded a special and equal dignity. But the document is strikingly silent overall on this implication, and the effect is that while it does cling to some concept of common humanity, it discards the ground of that concept. There must be a principle that distinguishes us from matter and justifies our claim to special dignity, and we cannot effectively assert that distinction without acknowledging its transcendent source—a being beyond.

Silence on this point might be understandable under certain circumstances—we are not always obliged to speak fully of the deepest things. But when the community of nations summons its best effort to state before the people of the world the true nature and source of the particular rights that it exists to protect, the only explanation for silence regarding that source is the fact that the members of the community disagree about it. Omission in the Universal Declaration of any mention of the authority of God, which is the true source of all human rights, is a confession of the fundamental disagreement of moral vision among the signatories.

Without the clear statement that rights come from God and must be respected out of respect for the authority of God, the Universal Declaration permits the impression that the list of rights it contains is a laundry list agreed upon by human will. And precisely because the countries signing the document were in disagreement about the actual source of those rights, it has proven impossible to attain consistent support for the authentic rights in the list, coherent understanding of what the various rights are and require, or any rational basis for preserving the list from arbitrary, spurious or even harmful additions.

Perhaps it would be helpful to contrast this situation with the American founding. The Declaration of Independence makes mention of fewer specific rights than the Universal Declaration, but it is absolutely clear about the source of those rights—the will of God as discovered by man in the self-evident truth of human equality. It might appear that this central principle of the American Declaration is less helpful to a people seeking justice than a list of rights that can be particularly pursued. But this is to miss the point of the Declaration of Independence.

In declaring that human equality under God is the self-evident truth that grounds all political judgment, the Declaration makes explicit for the American people what is already the actual basis for their deliberations about the requirements of justice. That is to say that the Declaration of Independence is the public and formal expression of the shared moral vision that really constitutes the American people. It is like a marriage vow—a public and formal commitment to a reality already acknowledged and fully intended.

Because the American Declaration speaks truly when it says that the American people "hold these truths to be self-evident," it needn't go on to list the conclusions that follow from them. The people can, for the most part, be relied upon to conduct this reasoning. And indeed, the history of the American Republic is perhaps best understood as a continued reflection by the American people on the meaning of the principles of the Declaration and the particular requirements those principles impose on us in the changing circumstances of national life.

When a substantial section of the American people decided, in the course of the 19th century, that they would no longer accept the burden of justifying their way of life by appeal to the principles of the Declaration, the result was the Civil War. That great conflict confirmed what our founders knew, and what the founders of the United Nations seem to have forgotten—human communities cannot sustain peaceful existence indefinitely unless their common life is based on a true, and truly shared, moral vision.

In our time, we in America face a new form of this inescapable requirement. Along with most of the "advanced" Western world, we have tolerated a sustained attempt to discard the underlying structure of justice by removing God and His law from any role in public life. But without the discipline provided by that vision of eternal justice, the movement to advance human rights in America has arrived rapidly, for example, at the absurdity that the unborn have no human rights that must be respected.

This does not mean that the American regime is as flawed as that of the United Nations. In America, defenders of human dignity can still point to the founding principles of American life, summarized and enshrined in the Declaration and in more than two centuries of national effort to realize them more perfectly in practice. While the American community is certainly in danger of forgetting its own deepest principles, it is also quite possible that we will remember them, for they remain alive in millions of souls, and in many inherited institutions and practices that retain great strength and prominence in our national life. The pro-life movement in America has the great advantage of being aimed, above all, at prompting a national recollection of who we still really are. That movement can point to the Declaration and invite fellow citizens to come home to its eternal truths.

To what universally held principles, and to what universal customs and practices enshrining such principles, can the defenders of human dignity appeal in the United Nations? The global community does not, in fact, share a common moral vision, and the practices of the member states run the gamut from the saintly to the monstrous.

The Universal Declaration of Human Rights, and the United Nations itself, are in a way an enormous bluff. It is as though the founders decided that the moment was right for a large scale effort at pretending that moral agreement existed where it really did not. The hope was that the bluff could be sustained long enough that the dissenting nations could be brought into line.

The bluff has failed, and predictably so. The Soviet Union, for instance, was both a principled opponent of the Western moral vision and an experienced deceiver. Offered the opportunity to be treated as a member of the world "community," the Soviet Union gladly accepted, and proceeded to strive mightily for decades to undermine that would-be community from within. And there were plenty of other nations— less potent in their evil but no more susceptible to the mild and confused moral encouragement the United Nations offered—who were also willing to sign documents and otherwise participate in the fiction of a global moral agreement as long as it was useful to their own national and tyrannical interests.

When we promise ourselves we will be good, and then try to live up to this commitment, we can sometimes generate a kind of moral momentum as we strive to make good on our promise to ourselves. The American Founding was perhaps such a moment of promise in the life of a people, and we have spent the last two centuries striving to live up to the promises we made in the Declaration to ourselves and to the world. Again and again we have reflected on what that document said we believed, and have turned back to our practical challenges with new resolve to live up to that original commitment.

At the American Founding, the formal commitment to seek justice was made out of a reasonable confidence that the moral resources to fulfill that commitment existed in the hearts of the American people. The formal commitment crystallized a resolve that was latent in the founding generation and brought to the surface by the circumstances of the Revolution and the requirement of justifying our decision to go to war to gain our independence.

The United Nations and the Universal Declaration of Human Rights are a different case entirely. The experience of 50 years has shown what should have been clear from the beginning—the labor to fulfill our promises to ourselves cannot be successful if we invite systematically vicious nations to help. We will inevitably lower both our explicit standards and our implicit expectations for their fulfillment, and we will lose our capacity to even remember the goal of justice itself. Prudence should have dictated then, and dictates now, that we concentrate on identifying and encouraging those beachheads of political truth that exist in the world, and on seeking first to form international communities among those nations that are forthright and sincere in their acknowledgment of moral truth.

The vision of human dignity and the task of accomplishing justice are truly universal. As Americans, we are heirs of that vision which declared human equality to be self-evident. It is always "our business" how the goal of respect for that equality is faring in the world. Prudence will usually dictate that we aid the cause of justice more by way of example and exhortation than by direct connection. Humility, too, will caution us against grand schemes in the world when we are not yet ourselves fulfilling the demands of justice at home.

But just as the American Republic arose not from grand schemes of national organization and political structure, but from the habits and virtues of the people themselves in their local communities, so the effective approach to justice internationally will not be through global conferences and laboriously negotiated statements of "rights." It will be through the natural tendency of national communities of justice to cooperate with one another on a larger scale.

In this way we will not only be faithful to the demands of prudence—we will also fulfill our duty as a virtuous people. Rejecting empty visions of world unity that discard moral principle does not mean that we reject that universal vision of international justice and human dignity. It means instead that we understand that we must remove the beam in our own eye before concerning ourselves with the mote in our brother's eye. And it means that we will be patient because we know that the perfection of justice is not to be accomplished in our lifetimes, or indeed in this world. The unseemly hurry of the United Nations to bring the still hungry lions together with the lambs is not only imprudent—it just might be idolatrous. The final peace among the nations will come in God's good time, and by His hand. We labor toward that goal in faith, knowing that our best deeds can be but approximations of the perfect justice that only God can give.

This collection of papers is a careful and scholarly review of the wreckage that has resulted from the unfortunate mixture of charity, pride and imprudence that gave rise to the United Nations. A careful reading of these papers will provide a detailed inoculation against the ignorant self-congratulation that the fiftieth anniversary of the

Universal Declaration of Human Rights has unleashed, and prepare the serious reader for renewed attempts to work toward the justice that is the only foundation of real unity among men and nations.